THE AUSTRALIAN Women's Weekly

contents

While each country in the Mediterranean is unique, they all have something in common: their cuisine is inspired by the abundance of local fruits and vegetables, fresh fish and meats. And these recipes show how the people of the Mediterranean turn their simple produce into mouth-watering meals – from the traditional pastizzi of Malta, to the famous bolognese of Italy, and the sweet baklava of Greece. Flicking through these pages will help you feel the warmth of the Mediterranean from your own home.

Pamela Clark

Food Director

chicken and rice soup

preparation time 10 minutes cooking time 25 minutes serves 6

2.25 litres (9 cups) chicken stock
½ cup (100g) white short-grain rice
3 eggs, separated
⅓ cup (80ml) lemon juice

1 Bring stock to a boil in large saucepan, add rice; cook, stirring occasionally, 15 minutes or until rice is tender. Reduce heat to lowest possible setting.
2 Working quickly, beat egg whites in small bowl with electric mixer until soft peaks form. Add yolks; continue beating until combined. With motor operating, gradually add lemon juice and 1 cup of the hot stock, beating until combined.
3 Remove stock mixture from heat; gradually add egg mixture, stirring constantly. Serve soup immediately.

SERVING SUGGESTION Serve as a first course, followed by a Greek braised lamb and vegetable main.
A cup of finely shredded poached chicken breast meat can be added to this soup, if desired.

SOUPS & STARTERS

vegetable soup with cheese

preparation time 25 minutes cooking time 50 minutes serves 6

2 teaspoons olive oil

1 medium brown onion (150g), chopped finely

2 cloves garlic, crushed

1 trimmed celery stalk (100g), chopped coarsely

1 large carrot (180g), chopped coarsely

1 litre (4 cups) vegetable stock

1 cup (250ml) water

810g can crushed tomatoes

1 medium zucchini (120g), chopped coarsely

2 cups (160g) finely shredded cabbage

150g small shell pasta

300g can white beans, rinsed, drained

¼ cup coarsely chopped fresh flat-leaf parsley

¾ cup (60g) shaved parmesan cheese

1 Heat oil in large saucepan; cook onion and garlic, stirring, until onion softens. Add celery and carrot; cook, stirring, 5 minutes.

2 Stir in stock, the water and undrained tomatoes; bring to a boil. Reduce heat; simmer, covered, about 20 minutes or until vegetables are tender.

3 Add zucchini, cabbage, pasta and beans to pan; cook, uncovered, about 15 minutes or until pasta is tender. Stir in parsley.

4 Serve soup topped with cheese.

Pastizzi are a traditional Maltese food. These flakey pastry pockets are traditionally filled with either fresh ricotta or mushy peas, but nowadays, the variety of fillings are endless and can be sweet or savoury. Fillings are usually distinguished by the unique shape: ricotta-filled pastizzi are diamond shaped; pea-filled pastizzi are a rounded semi-circle. It is common for the Maltese to have pastizzi on hand in the freezer; as they usually make them in bulk and freeze the raw pastizzi until required.

pastizzi tar-rikotta (cheese cakes)

preparation time 15 minutes cooking time 30 minutes makes 24

6 sheets ready rolled puff pastry (1kg)

1 egg, beaten lightly

500g ricotta cheese

1 Preheat oven to 220°C/200°C fan-forced. Oil oven trays.
2 Cut each pastry sheet into four squares. Brush egg on two opposing sides of a pastry square; place 2 level tablespoons of ricotta along centre of square. Bring egg-brushed sides together, pinching ends to seal.
3 Place on trays; bake about 30 minutes or until golden brown.

pastizzi tal-pizelli (pea pastizzi)

preparation time 15 minutes cooking time 30 minutes makes 24

500g frozen peas

20g butter

1 small brown onion (80g), chopped finely

170g can corned beef

½ teaspoon curry powder

6 sheets ready rolled puff pastry (1kg)

1 egg, beaten lightly

1 Preheat oven to 220°C/200°C fan-forced. Oil oven trays.
2 Place peas in large saucepan, and add enough water to just cover. Boil peas about 20 minutes or until very soft; drain.
3 Heat butter in large frying pan; cook onion until soft. Add peas, corned beef and curry powder. Stir mixture until heated through, mashing with fork so peas break down. Remove from heat; cool.
4 Cut rounds from pastry sheets using 10cm cutter (you need 24 rounds). Brush rounds lightly with egg; place 1 rounded tablespoon of pea mixture in centre. Fold in half to enclose filling; press edges to seal and fold slightly.
5 Place on trays; bake about 30 minutes or until golden brown.

vegetable soup with risoni

preparation time 15 minutes cooking time 2 hours serves 6

4 litres (16 cups) water

3 large carrots (540g), chopped coarsely

2 large brown onions (400g), chopped coarsely

4 trimmed celery stalks (400g), chopped coarsely

1 tablespoon black peppercorns

4 bay leaves

10 sprigs fresh flat-leaf parsley

1 tablespoon olive oil

1 large brown onion (200g), chopped coarsely, extra

2 cloves garlic, crushed

150g pancetta, chopped coarsely

2 medium carrots (240g), chopped coarsely, extra

2 medium potatoes (400g), chopped coarsely

2 sprigs fresh rosemary

1 cup (220g) risoni

¼ cup coarsely chopped fresh flat-leaf parsley, extra

1 Combine the water, carrot, onion, celery, peppercorns, bay leaves and parsley in large saucepan; bring to a boil. Reduce heat; simmer, uncovered, 1½ hours; strain over large bowl. Reserve stock; discard vegetables. [Can be made ahead to this stage. Cover; refrigerate overnight or freeze.]

2 Heat oil in large saucepan; cook extra onion, garlic and pancetta, stirring, until onion is soft. Add extra carrot, potato and rosemary; cook, stirring, 5 minutes. Stir in stock; bring to a boil. Reduce heat; simmer, uncovered, about 10 minutes or until vegetables are tender.

3 Stir in pasta, bring to a boil. Reduce heat; simmer, uncovered, about 5 minutes or until risoni is just tender. Stir in extra parsley.

This recipe can be made up to 2 days ahead and stored, covered, in the refrigerator. Be sure to remove and discard any solidified fat from the surface of the cooled broth. If the cooled broth is to be kept longer than that, freeze it.

beef broth

preparation time 15 minutes **cooking time** 5 hours **makes** about 2.5 litres (10 cups)

2kg meaty beef bones

2 medium brown onions (300g)

2 trimmed celery stalks (200g), chopped coarsely

2 medium carrots (250g), chopped coarsely

3 bay leaves

2 teaspoons black peppercorns

5 litres (20 cups) water

3 litres (12 cups) water, extra

1 Preheat oven to 220°C/200°C fan-forced.

2 Place bones and unpeeled coarsely chopped onions in baking dish. Roast, uncovered, about 1 hour or until bones and onions are well browned.

3 Transfer bones and onions to large saucepan; add celery, carrot, bay leaves, peppercorns and the water. Simmer, uncovered, 3 hours, skimming surface occasionally.

4 Add the extra water; simmer, uncovered, 1 hour, skimming surface occasionally. Strain broth mixture through muslin-lined strainer into large clean bowl.

lamb and vegetable broth

preparation time 30 minutes **cooking time** 1 hour 40 minutes **serves** 4

1kg lamb neck chops

2.25 litres (9 cups) water

¾ cup (150g) pearl barley

1 large brown onion (200g), diced into 1cm pieces

2 medium carrots (240g), diced into 1cm pieces

1 medium leek (350g), sliced thinly

2 cups (160g) finely shredded savoy cabbage

½ cup (60g) frozen peas

2 tablespoons coarsely chopped fresh flat-leaf parsley

1 Combine chops with the water and barley in large saucepan; bring to a boil. Reduce heat, simmer, covered, 1 hour, skimming fat from surface occasionally. Add onion, carrot and leek; simmer, covered, about 30 minutes or until vegetables are tender.

2 Remove chops from soup mixture; when cool enough to handle, remove meat, chop coarsely. Discard bones.

3 Return meat to soup with cabbage and peas; cook, uncovered, about 10 minutes or until cabbage is tender. Sprinkle parsley over broth just before serving.

pumpkin soup

preparation time 20 minutes cooking time 35 minutes serves 6

40g butter

1 large brown onion (200g), chopped coarsely

1.5kg pumpkin, chopped coarsely

2 large potatoes (600g), chopped coarsely

1.5 litres (6 cups) chicken stock

½ cup (125ml) cream

1   Melt butter in large saucepan; cook onion, stirring, until soft. Stir in pumpkin and potato; cook, stirring, 5 minutes.

2   Stir in stock, bring to a boil. Reduce heat; simmer, uncovered, about 20 minutes or until pumpkin is soft, stirring occasionally.

3   Blend or process soup, in batches, until pureed; push through food mill or large sieve into large clean saucepan. [Can be made ahead to this stage. Cover; refrigerate overnight or freeze.]

4   Just before serving, add cream; stir over heat until soup is hot. Serve topped with a dollop of sour cream and a few chives, if desired.

TIP Pushing the soup through a food mill or a sieve after the initial blending or processing results in an almost velvet-smooth texture.

SNAILS IN GREEN SAUCE

snails in green sauce

preparation time 10 minutes cooking time 20 minutes serves 4 to 6

1 tablespoon olive oil

1 small onion (80g), finely chopped

4 cloves garlic, crushed

1 teaspoon plain flour

2 tablespoons dry white wine

¼ cup (60 ml) fish stock

2 tablespoons cream

¼ cup chopped fresh flat-leaf parsley

24 large canned snails with shells, drained

rock salt

1 Preheat oven to 220°C/200°C fan-forced.

2 Heat oil in small saucepan; cook onion and garlic, stirring, until onion is soft. Add flour, stir over heat until bubbling.

3 Gradually stir in combined wine, stock and cream; stir over heat until sauce boils and thickens. Stir in parsley.

4 Push the snails into shells; spoon sauce into shells. Arrange shells on rock salt, in shallow ovenproof dish. Bake, uncovered, for about 5 minutes or until heated through.

TIP You will need the snail's shells for this recipe.

snails in garlic butter

preparation time 10 minutes cooking time 10 minutes serves 2

90g butter

2 cloves garlic, crushed

2 tablespoons chopped fresh flat-leaf parsley

30g butter, extra

1 clove garlic, crushed, extra

½ cup (35 g) fresh breadcrumbs

220g can snails with shells, drained

1 Preheat oven to 180°C/160°C fan-forced.

2 Melt butter in small saucepan, stir in garlic and parsley.

3 In another small saucepan, melt extra butter; cook breadcrumbs and extra garlic, stirring, over medium heat 1 minute. Remove from heat.

4 Dip each snail in garlic butter and place in shells, place ½ teaspoon of breadcrumb mixture on top. Bake, uncovered, for 5 to 8 minutes. Serve remaining garlic butter separately.

This is a great prepare-ahead soup which can be frozen after the processing or blending step. Defrost in the refrigerator and, just before serving, add the cream and thyme, then reheat.

TIP The smoothest consistency for this soup will be achieved by using a blender, stab mixer or mouli.

pea and potato soup

preparation time 5 minutes **cooking time** 25 minutes **serves** 4

30g butter

1 small leek (200g), sliced thinly

2 trimmed celery stalks (200g), chopped coarsely

3 large potatoes (900g), chopped coarsely

3 cups (750ml) vegetable stock

2 cups (500ml) water

2 cups (250g) frozen peas

⅓ cup (80ml) cream

1 tablespoon fresh thyme

1 Melt butter in large saucepan; cook leek and celery, stirring, until vegetables soften.

2 Add potato, stock and the water. Cover; bring to a boil. Reduce heat, simmer, stirring occasionally, 15 minutes or until potato softens.

3 Add peas; cook, uncovered, about 5 minutes or until peas are tender.

4 Blend or process soup, in batches, until smooth; return to pan. Add cream and thyme; stir until hot.

SERVING SUGGESTION Serve with herb scones or crusty bread.

SOUPS & STARTERS

20

bean soup

preparation time 25 minutes (plus soaking and standing time) cooking time 1 hour 40 minutes serves 4

1½ cups (300g) dried haricot beans

1 tablespoon olive oil

1 medium brown onion (150g), chopped coarsely

2 cloves garlic, crushed

2 trimmed celery stalks (200g), chopped coarsely

1 medium carrot (120g), chopped coarsely

2 rindless bacon rashers (125g), chopped coarsely

4 large ripe tomatoes (1kg), peeled, chopped coarsely

1.5 litres (6 cups) vegetable stock

1 teaspoon sugar

¼ cup fresh flat-leaf parsley sprigs

¼ cup (70g) tomato paste

1 Cover beans with water in large bowl; stand, covered, overnight.
2 Heat oil in large saucepan; cook onion, garlic, celery, carrot and bacon, stirring, until vegetables are just tender.
3 Add tomato; cook, stirring, about 5 minutes or until tomato is soft.
4 Stir in rinsed drained beans, stock, sugar, parsley and paste; bring to a boil. Reduce heat, simmer, covered, about 1½ hours or until beans are tender.

TIP This recipe can be made a day ahead and refrigerated, covered, or frozen for up to 2 months..

tomato and bread soup

preparation time 30 minutes cooking time 45 minutes serves 6

100g piece ciabatta bread, cut into 2cm slices

1 tablespoon olive oil

2 large brown onions (400g), chopped finely

3 cloves garlic, crushed

2kg tomatoes, peeled, chopped coarsely

2 litres (8 cups) vegetable stock

2 tablespoons tomato paste

1 teaspoon sugar

¼ cup coarsely chopped fresh basil

1 Preheat oven to 220°C/200°C fan-forced.
2 Place bread on oven tray; bake, uncovered, about 10 minutes or until crisp. [Can be made 2 days ahead to this stage; store in an airtight container.]
3 Heat oil in large saucepan; cook onion and garlic, stirring, until onion is soft. Add tomato; cook, stirring occasionally, about 10 minutes or until tomato is pulpy.
4 Break bread into large pieces directly into pan. Add stock, paste and sugar; simmer, uncovered, about 15 minutes or until soup thickens slightly. Stir occasionally to break up any bread pieces. Just before serving, stir in basil.
5 Drizzle with extra virgin olive oil, if desired.

TIP Any leftover stale bread having a hard, crunchy crust can be substituted for ciabatta, if unavailable.

meatballs with chilli mushroom sauce

preparation time 15 minutes cooking time 20 minutes serves 4

500g pork and veal mince

1 cup (70g) stale breadcrumbs

¼ cup finely chopped fresh oregano

3 cloves garlic, crushed

⅓ cup (95g) tomato paste

1 egg, beaten lightly

1 tablespoon olive oil

250g button mushrooms, sliced thinly

850g canned tomatoes

¼ cup (60ml) mild chilli sauce

1 Preheat oven to 200°C/180°C fan-forced. Oil oven tray.

2 Combine mince, breadcrumbs, oregano, garlic, paste and egg in medium bowl. Roll level tablespoons of mixture into balls; place on tray. Bake, uncovered, about 15 minutes or until cooked through.

3 Meanwhile, heat oil in large saucepan; cook mushrooms, stirring, until just soft. Add undrained crushed tomatoes and sauce to pan; bring to a boil. Reduce heat, simmer, uncovered, 5 minutes. Add meatballs; cook, stirring, 2 minutes.

STORE Recipe can be made 2 days ahead and refrigerated, covered, or frozen for up to 3 months.

veal rolls with rice and peas

preparation time 25 minutes cooking time 40 minutes serves 4

8 slices pancetta (120g)

8 veal schnitzels (800g)

²/₃ cup (100g) drained sun-dried tomatoes in oil, sliced thinly

⅓ cup (55g) seeded green olives, sliced thinly

1 tablespoon drained baby capers, rinsed

2 teaspoons fresh marjoram leaves

1 tablespoon olive oil

RICE AND PEAS

1 litre (4 cups) water

2 cups (500ml) chicken stock

40g butter

2 cups (400g) arborio rice

1 cup (125g) frozen baby peas

1 cup (80g) finely grated parmesan cheese

¼ cup finely chopped fresh flat-leaf parsley

1   Preheat oven to 180°C/160°C fan-forced.

2   Place one slice of pancetta on each schnitzel; divide tomato, olives, capers and marjoram between schnitzels.

3   Roll schnitzels to enclose filling; tie with kitchen string to secure.

4   Start making rice and peas.

5   Heat oil in large frying pan; cook braciole, uncovered, until browned all over. Place on oven tray; bake, uncovered, about 10 minutes or until cooked through.

6   Serve veal rolls with rice and peas.

RICE AND PEAS Place the water and stock in medium saucepan; bring to a boil. Reduce heat, simmer, covered. Melt butter in large saucepan, add rice; stir until rice is coated in butter and slightly opaque. Stir in 1 cup of the hot stock mixture; cook, stirring, over low heat, until liquid is absorbed. Continue adding stock mixture, in 1-cup batches, stirring until absorbed after each addition. Add peas with last cup of stock mixture; stir in cheese and parsley.

beef, tomato and pea pies

preparation time 15 minutes (plus refrigeration time) **cooking time** 45 minutes (plus cooling time) **makes** 6

1 tablespoon vegetable oil

1 small brown onion (80g), chopped finely

300g beef mince

400g can tomatoes

1 tablespoon tomato paste

2 tablespoons worcestershire sauce

½ cup (125ml) beef stock

½ cup (60g) frozen peas

3 sheets ready-rolled puff pastry

1 egg, beaten lightly

1 Heat oil in large saucepan; cook onion, stirring, until softened. Add beef; cook, stirring, until changed in colour. Stir in undrained crushed tomatoes, paste, sauce and stock; bring to a boil. Reduce heat, simmer, uncovered, about 20 minutes or until sauce thickens. Stir in peas. Cool.

2 Preheat oven to 200°C/180°C fan-forced. Oil six-hole (¾ cup/180ml) Texas muffin pan.

3 Cut two 13cm rounds from opposite corners of each pastry sheet; cut two 9cm rounds from remaining corners of each sheet. Place the six large rounds in muffin pan holes to cover bases and sides; trim any excess pastry. Lightly prick bases with fork; refrigerate 30 minutes. Cover the six small rounds with a damp cloth.

4 Cover pastry-lined muffin pan holes with baking paper; fill holes with uncooked rice or dried beans. Bake, uncovered, 10 minutes; remove paper and rice. Cool.

5 Spoon mince filling into holes; brush edges with a little egg. Top pies with small pastry rounds; gently press around edges to seal.

6 Brush pies with remaining egg; bake, uncovered, further 15 minutes or until browned lightly. Stand 5 minutes in pan before serving with mashed potato, if desired.

beef in red wine

preparation time 15 minutes cooking time 1¼ hours serves 2

350g beef blade steak

2 medium brown onions (300g), chopped finely

1 clove garlic, crushed

100g mushrooms, sliced thickly

415ml can tomato puree

2 teaspoons worcestershire sauce

½ cup (125ml) dry red wine

1 trimmed celery stalk (100g), chopped coarsely

2 medium carrots (240g), chopped coarsely

2 tablespoons fresh flat-leaf parsley leaves

1 Trim all visible fat from steak; cut steak into cubes. Cook steak in heated large saucepan until browned all over.

2 Add onion, garlic and mushrooms; cook, stirring, for about 2 minutes or until onion is soft. Stir in puree, sauce and wine; bring to a boil. Reduce heat, simmer, covered, about 45 minutes.

3 Add celery and carrot; cook, covered, further 15 minutes or until vegetables are tender. Serve sprinkled with parsley and accompanied with couscous, if desired.

STORE Recipe can be made a day ahead and refrigerated, covered.

beef and onion kebabs

preparation time 20 minutes (plus refrigeration time) cooking time 10 minutes serves 2

350g lean rump steak

9 baby onions (225g), halved

MARINADE

¼ cup (60ml) honey

¼ cup (60ml) lemon juice

2 teaspoons grated fresh ginger

2 teaspoons worcestershire sauce

¼ cup (60ml) tomato sauce

1 tablespoon finely chopped fresh oregano

1 Remove all visible fat from steak; chop steak into bite-size pieces. Thread steak and onion onto six skewers. Place in shallow dish.

2 Make marinade; pour over kebabs. Cover; refrigerate overnight.

3 Cook kebabs on heated grill pan (or grill or barbecue), brushing with marinade, until meat is tender. Serve with bitter leaf salad, if desired.
MARINADE Combine all ingredients in bowl; mix well.

TIP Cook marinated kebabs just before serving.

roasted lamb with lemon potatoes

preparation time 25 minutes (plus refrigeration time) cooking time 1 hour 50 minutes serves 6

¼ cup (60ml) olive oil

2 tablespoons grated lemon rind

2 tablespoons lemon juice

2 tablespoons dry white wine

2 teaspoons seasoned pepper

2 tablespoons chopped fresh thyme

2kg leg of lamb

2 cloves garlic, sliced

1 tablespoon fresh rosemary leaves

LEMON POTATOES

12 medium old potatoes (2.4kg)

¼ cup (60ml) olive oil

⅓ cup (80ml) lemon juice

1½ tablespoons grated lemon rind

2 tablespoons chopped fresh rosemary

2 tablespoons chopped fresh thyme

1½ teaspoons cracked black pepper

1 Combine oil, rind, juice, wine, pepper and thyme in medium jug; mix well. Trim excess fat from lamb. Using point of knife, make 12 incisions evenly over top of lamb leg. Place a slice of garlic and some of the rosemary leaves in each incision. Pour oil mixture over lamb, cover; refrigerate, turning lamb occasionally, 3 hours or overnight.

2 Preheat oven to 200°C/180°C fan-forced.

3 Drain lamb, reserve marinade. Place lamb in large baking dish; bake, uncovered, 40 minutes.

4 Make lemon potatoes; add to baking dish with lamb. Bake further 50 minutes, turning occasionally, or until lamb and potatoes are tender. Remove lamb from baking dish, cover, keep warm. Drain juices from dish; reserve juices.

5 Increase oven temperature to 240°C/220°C fan-forced. Bake potatoes further 20 minutes or until browned and crisp; remove from dish, cover, keep warm.

6 Heat reserved marinade and reserved juices in dish, bring to a boil; serve with sliced lamb, lemon potatoes and, if desired, steamed green beans.
   LEMON POTATOES Cut potatoes into 3cm pieces, place in bowl, pour over combined remaining ingredients; mix well.

osso buco with semi-dried tomatoes and olives

preparation time 30 minutes cooking time 2 hours 45 minutes serves 6

12 pieces veal osso buco (3kg)

¼ cup (35g) plain flour

¼ cup (60ml) olive oil

40g butter

1 medium brown onion (150g),
chopped coarsely

2 cloves garlic, chopped finely

3 trimmed celery stalks (300g),
chopped coarsely

2 large carrots (360g), chopped coarsely

4 medium tomatoes (600g),
chopped coarsely

2 tablespoons tomato paste

1 cup (250ml) dry white wine

1 cup (250ml) beef stock

400g can crushed tomatoes

4 sprigs fresh lemon thyme

½ cup (75g) drained semi-dried tomatoes

¼ cup (60ml) lemon juice

1 tablespoon finely grated lemon rind

½ cup (75g) seeded kalamata olives

GREMOLATA

1 tablespoon finely grated lemon rind

⅓ cup finely chopped fresh flat-leaf parsley

2 cloves garlic, chopped finely

1 Coat veal in flour; shake off excess. Heat oil in large deep saucepan; cook veal, in batches, until browned all over.

2 Melt butter in same pan; cook onion, garlic, celery and carrot, stirring, until vegetables just soften. Stir in fresh tomato, paste, wine, stock, undrained tomatoes and thyme. Return veal to pan, fitting pieces upright and tightly together in single layer; bring to a boil. Reduce heat, simmer, covered, 1¾ hours. Stir in semi-dried tomatoes; simmer, uncovered, 30 minutes or until veal is tender.

3 Meanwhile, make gremolata.

4 Remove veal from pan; cover to keep warm. Bring sauce to a boil; boil, uncovered, about 10 minutes or until sauce thickens slightly. Stir in juice, rind and olives.

5 Divide veal among serving plates; top with sauce, sprinkle with gremolata. Serve with soft polenta, if desired.
   GREMOLATA Combine ingredients in small bowl.

chicken drumsticks with olives and artichokes

preparation time 15 minutes cooking time 1 hour serves 4

2 tablespoons olive oil

12 chicken drumsticks (1.8kg)

1 medium white onion (150g), chopped finely

3 cloves garlic, crushed

1 tablespoon finely grated lemon rind

1½ cups (375ml) chicken stock

½ cup (125ml) dry white wine

340g jar marinated artichokes,
drained, quartered

500g risoni

2 tablespoons finely chopped fresh oregano

1 cup (150g) seeded kalamata olives

1 tablespoon finely grated lemon rind, extra

¼ cup (60ml) lemon juice

1   Heat half of the oil in large saucepan; cook drumsticks, in batches, until browned all over.

2   Heat remaining oil in same pan; cook onion and garlic, stirring, until onion softens. Add rind, stock, wine and artichokes; bring to a boil. Return drumsticks to pan; reduce heat, simmer, covered, 20 minutes. Uncover; simmer, further 10 minutes or until drumsticks are cooked through.

3   Meanwhile, cook risoni in large saucepan of boiling water, uncovered, until just tender; drain.

4   Remove chicken from pan; stir oregano, olives, extra juice and extra rind into sauce.

5   Serve chicken with sauce on risoni.

POULTRY & RABBIT

chicken stuffed with couscous

preparation time 30 minutes cooking time 2 hours 20 minutes (plus standing time) **serves** 4

1.6kg chicken

20g butter, melted

20 baby vine-ripened truss tomatoes (400g)

1 tablespoon olive oil

COUSCOUS STUFFING

1 teaspoon olive oil

1 medium brown onion (150g), chopped finely

1½ cups (375ml) chicken stock

¼ cup (60ml) olive oil, extra

1 tablespoon finely grated lemon rind

¼ cup (60ml) lemon juice

1 cup (200g) couscous

½ cup (70g) toasted slivered almonds

1 cup (140g) seeded dried dates, chopped finely

1 teaspoon ground cinnamon

1 teaspoon smoked paprika

1 egg, beaten lightly

GREEN OLIVE SALSA

1½ cups (180g) seeded green olives,
chopped coarsely

⅓ cup (80ml) olive oil

1 tablespoon cider vinegar

1 shallot (25g), chopped finely

1 fresh long red chilli, chopped finely

¼ cup coarsely chopped fresh flat-leaf parsley

¼ cup coarsely chopped fresh mint

1 Make couscous stuffing.

2 Preheat oven to 200°C/180°C fan-forced.

3 Wash chicken under cold water; pat dry inside and out with absorbent paper. Fill large cavity loosely with couscous stuffing; tie legs together with kitchen string.

4 Half fill a large baking dish with water; place chicken on oiled wire rack over dish. Brush chicken all over with butter; roast, uncovered, 15 minutes. Reduce oven to 180°C/160°C fan-forced; roast, uncovered, about 1½ hours or until cooked through. Remove chicken from rack; cover, stand 20 minutes.

5 Meanwhile, place tomatoes on oven tray; drizzle with oil. Roast, uncovered, about 20 minutes or until softened and browned lightly.

6 Make green olive salsa.

7 Serve chicken with tomatoes and salsa.
   COUSCOUS STUFFING Heat oil in small frying pan; cook onion, stirring, until onion is soft. Combine stock, extra oil, rind and juice in medium saucepan; bring to a boil. Remove from heat. Add couscous, cover; stand about 5 minutes or until stock is absorbed, fluffing with fork occasionally. Stir in onion, nuts, dates, spices and egg.
   GREEN OLIVE SALSA Combine all ingredients in small bowl.

hearty rabbit stew

preparation time 15 minutes cooking time 1¼ hours serves 2

2 teaspoons olive oil

6 spring onions

400g rabbit pieces

1 tablespoon plain flour

¾ cup (180ml) water

½ cup (125ml) dry white wine

2 teaspoons tomato paste

4 baby potatoes (270g), quartered

175g baby carrots, trimmed

60g sugar snap peas

1 Heat half of the oil in large saucepan; cook onions, stirring, for about 3 minutes or until brown all over. Set aside.
2 Toss rabbit in flour. Heat remaining oil in same pan; cook rabbit until browned all over.
3 Stir in the water, wine and paste; bring to a boil. Reduce heat, simmer, covered, for 45 minutes.
4 Add potato and onion; cook further 15 minutes. Add carrot and peas; cook until vegetables are tender.

STORE Recipe can be made a day ahead and refrigerated, covered.

rabbit and tomato casserole

preparation time 10 minutes cooking time 1 hour serves 2

400g rabbit pieces

1 large brown onion (200g), chopped finely

200g pumpkin, chopped coarsely

½ medium red capsicum (100g), chopped finely

410g can tomatoes

1 clove garlic, crushed

½ cup (125ml) dry white wine

½ cup (125ml) water

2 tablespoons coarsely chopped fresh flat-leaf parsley

1 Cook rabbit in heated large saucepan until browned all over. Add onion; cook, stirring, until onion is soft.

2 Add remaining ingredients, except parsley, to pan; bring to a boil. Reduce heat, simmer, covered, for about 45 minutes or until rabbit is tender. Sprinkle with parsley to serve.

STORE Recipe can be made a day ahead and refrigerated, covered.

chicken parmigiana

preparation time 10 minutes cooking time 20 minutes serves 4

2 chicken breast fillets (400g)

2 tablespoons plain flour

1 egg

1 tablespoon milk

1 cup (70g) stale breadcrumbs

¼ cup (60ml) vegetable oil

⅓ cup (85g) bottled tomato pasta sauce, warmed

4 slices leg ham (185g)

100g gruyère cheese, grated coarsely

1 Preheat grill.

2 Split chicken fillets in half horizontally. Toss chicken in flour; shake away excess. Dip chicken pieces, one at a time, in combined egg and milk, then in breadcrumbs.

3 Heat oil in large frying pan; shallow-fry chicken, in batches, until browned and cooked through. Drain on absorbent paper.

4 Place chicken on oven tray; divide pasta sauce, then top with ham and cheese. Place under grill until cheese melts.

SERVING SUGGESTION Serve with a parmesan and baby rocket salad, if desired.

barbecued lemon thyme chicken

preparation time 25 minutes cooking time 1 hour 20 minutes (plus standing time) serves 4

6 cloves garlic, sliced thickly

3 shallots (75g), chopped finely

½ cup (125ml) chicken stock

20g butter, softened

1 tablespoon finely chopped
fresh lemon thyme

1.6kg chicken

600g kipfler potatoes, halved lengthways

340g asparagus, trimmed

1 medium lemon (140g), quartered

1 tablespoon olive oil

1   Place garlic, shallot and stock in small saucepan; bring to a boil. Reduce heat, simmer, uncovered, about 20 minutes or until garlic is soft and liquid is almost evaporated. Cool 5 minutes; stir in butter and thyme.

2   Wash chicken under cold water; pat dry inside and out with absorbent paper. Using kitchen scissors, cut along each side of backbone; discard backbone. Place chicken, skin-side up, on board. Using heel of hand, press down on breastbone to flatten chicken. Make a pocket between chicken and skin; push thyme mixture under skin.

3   Cook chicken, skin-side down, on heated oiled grill plate (or grill or barbecue), covered, over medium heat, 15 minutes. Turn; cook, covered, about 35 minutes or until cooked through. Cover; stand 15 minutes.

4   Meanwhile, boil, steam or microwave potato until just tender; drain. Cook potato, asparagus and lemon on same grill plate (or grill or barbecue) brushing with oil, until browned.

5   Serve chicken with potato, asparagus and lemon.

Muscat is a sweet, aromatic dessert wine, possessing an almost musty flavour. It is made from the fully matured muscatel grape.

roast bacon-wrapped quail with muscat sauce

preparation time 15 minutes cooking time 30 minutes serves 4

4 quails (780g)

1 lemon

20g butter

4 rindless bacon rashers (250g)

⅓ cup (80ml) muscat

250g green beans

½ cup (125ml) chicken stock

150g fresh muscatel grapes, halved

1 Preheat oven to 200°C/180°C fan-froced.

2 Discard necks from quails. Wash quails under cold water; pat dry with absorbent paper.

3 Halve lemon; cut one lemon half into four wedges. Place one lemon wedge and a quarter of the butter inside each quail. Tuck legs along body, wrapping tightly with bacon rasher to hold legs in place.

4 Place quails in medium flameproof casserole dish; drizzle with 1 tablespoon of the muscat and juice of remaining lemon half. Roast, uncovered, about 25 minutes or until quails are browned and cooked through. Remove quails from dish; cover to keep warm.

5 Meanwhile, boil, steam or microwave beans until tender; drain. Cover to keep warm.

6 Return dish with pan liquid to heat, add remaining muscat and stock; stir until sauce boils and reduces to about ½ cup. Add grapes; stir until heated though. Serve quail on beans topped with muscat sauce.

quail with polenta

preparation time 25 minutes (plus refrigeration time) cooking time 55 minutes serves 4

8 quail (1.6kg)

2 teaspoons olive oil

5 slices pancetta (75g), chopped coarsely

1 tablespoon pine nuts

¼ cup (60ml) brandy

¼ cup (40g) raisins

1¾ cups (430ml) chicken stock

MARINADE

½ cup (125ml) olive oil

1 tablespoon coarsely chopped fresh rosemary

2 teaspoons coarsely chopped fresh thyme

1 tablespoon finely shredded lemon rind

POLENTA

1½ cups (375ml) chicken stock

½ cup (85g) polenta

30g butter, melted

¼ cup (20g) grated parmesan cheese

2 tablespoons polenta, extra

olive oil for shallow-frying

1   Remove and discard necks from quail. Using kitchen scissors, cut through either side of backbone; discard backbone. Cut quail in half. Rinse quail under cold running water; pat dry with absorbent paper. Place quail in large shallow non-reactive dish.

2   Combine marinade ingredients in small bowl; pour over quail. Cover; refrigerate 3 hours. [Can be made a day ahead to this stage.]

3   Meanwhile, make polenta.

4   Heat oil in large frying pan; cook drained quail, in batches, covered, 5 minutes. Turn quail; cook, covered, further 7 minutes or until well browned and tender. Keep warm.

5   Add pancetta and pine nuts to pan; cook, stirring, 2 minutes or until pine nuts are browned lightly. Add brandy and raisins; cook 2 minutes or until liquid reduces by half. Add stock; simmer, uncovered, about 5 minutes or until thickened slightly.

6   Serve quail with polenta and sauce.

POLENTA Bring stock to a boil in large saucepan. Gradually add polenta; simmer, stirring, about 10 minutes or until soft and thick. Stir in butter and cheese. Press firmly into oiled 17cm sandwich cake pan; cool. Refrigerate, covered, 3 hours. [Can be made a day ahead to this stage.] Turn cooked polenta out of pan; cut into wedges. Coat wedges in extra polenta. Heat oil in medium frying pan; shallow-fry polenta wedges until browned lightly.

chicken and mushroom bake

preparation time 20 minutes cooking time 30 minutes serves 4

375g rigatoni

60g butter

600g chicken breast fillets, diced into 1cm pieces

100g button mushrooms, sliced thinly

2 tablespoons plain flour

2 cups (500ml) milk

½ cup (40g) coarsely grated romano cheese

1¼ cups (150g) coarsely grated cheddar cheese

170g fresh asparagus, trimmed, chopped coarsely

¼ cup coarsely chopped fresh flat-leaf parsley

1 Preheat oven to 200°C/180°C fan-forced.

2 Cook pasta in large saucepan of boiling water, uncovered, until just tender; drain.

3 Meanwhile, heat a third of the butter in large frying pan; cook chicken, in batches, until browned and cooked through.

4 Heat remaining butter in same pan; cook mushrooms, stirring, until tender. Add flour; cook, stirring, 1 minute. Gradually stir in milk. Stir over medium heat until mixture boils and thickens. Stir in chicken, ¼ cup of the romano, ¾ cup of the cheddar and the asparagus.

5 Combine chicken mixture and drained pasta in 2.5 litre (10-cup) ovenproof dish; sprinkle with remaining cheeses. Bake, uncovered, about 15 minutes or until top browns lightly. Sprinkle with parsley and serve with a mixed green salad, if desired.

chicken and lentil cacciatore

preparation time 15 minutes cooking time 40 minutes serves 4

cooking-oil spray

8 skinless chicken thigh fillets (880g), halved

1 medium brown onion (150g), chopped finely

300g button mushrooms, halved

1 clove garlic, crushed

2 x 440g cans tomatoes

1 tablespoon tomato paste

1 cup (250ml) chicken stock

⅓ cup (65g) red lentils

½ cup (60g) seeded black olives

1 tablespoon drained capers

2 teaspoons finely chopped fresh oregano

2 tablespoons finely chopped fresh flat-leaf parsley

1 Lightly spray large non-stick saucepan with cooking-oil spray. Cook chicken until browned all over, turning occasionally. Remove from pan.

2 Add onion, mushroom and garlic to pan; cook, stirring, until onion is soft. Add undrained crushed tomatoes, paste, stock and lentils.

3 Return chicken to pan; simmer, covered, for about 30 minutes or until chicken is tender. Stir in olives, capers, oregano and parsley.

STORE Recipe can be made a day ahead and refrigerated, covered, or frozen.

We've used pork and chicken in our forcemeat stuffing, however, you can use your favourite mixture of fish, poultry, meat, vegetables or fruit with breadcrumbs and various seasonings. This recipe will serve between eight and 12 people depending on your menu.

TIP To test if turkey is cooked, insert a skewer sideways into the thickest part of the thigh then remove and press flesh to release the juices. If the juice runs clear, the turkey is cooked. Alternatively, insert a meat thermometer into the thickest part of the thigh, without touching bone; it should reach 90°C.

traditional turkey with forcemeat stuffing

preparation time 40 minutes cooking time 3 hours 10 minutes (plus standing time) serves 8 to 12

4.5kg turkey

1 cup (250ml) water

80g butter, melted

¼ cup (35g) plain flour

3 cups (750ml) chicken stock

½ cup (125ml) dry white wine

FORCEMEAT STUFFING

40g butter

3 medium brown onions (450g), chopped finely

2 rindless bacon rashers (125g), chopped coarsely

1 cup (70g) stale breadcrumbs

2 tablespoons finely chopped fresh tarragon

½ cup coarsely chopped fresh flat-leaf parsley

½ cup (75g) coarsely chopped roasted pistachios

250g pork mince

250g chicken mince

1 Make forcemeat stuffing.

2 Preheat oven to 180°C/160°C fan-forced.

3 Discard neck from turkey. Rinse turkey under cold water; pat dry inside and out with absorbent paper. Fill neck cavity loosely with stuffing; secure skin over opening with toothpicks. Fill large cavity loosely with stuffing; tie legs together with kitchen string.

4 Place turkey on oiled wire rack in large shallow flameproof baking dish; pour the water into dish. Brush turkey all over with half of the butter; cover dish tightly with two layers of greased foil. Roast 2 hours. Uncover turkey; brush with remaining butter. Roast, uncovered, about 45 minutes or until browned all over and cooked through. Remove turkey from dish, cover turkey; stand 20 minutes.

5 Pour juice from dish into large jug; skim 1 tablespoon of the fat from juice, return to same dish. Skim and discard remaining fat from juice. Add flour to dish; cook, stirring, until mixture bubbles and is well browned. Gradually stir in stock, wine and remaining juice; bring to a boil, stirring, until gravy boils and thickens. Strain gravy into same jug; serve turkey with gravy.

FORCEMEAT STUFFING Melt butter in medium frying pan; cook onion and bacon, stirring, until onion softens. Using hand, combine onion mixture in large bowl with remaining ingredients.

mussels with garlic crumbs

preparation time 20 minutes cooking time 10 minutes serves 8

1 cup (70g) stale breadcrumbs

2 cloves garlic, chopped finely

1 teaspoon finely grated lemon rind

2 tablespoons finely chopped
fresh flat-leaf parsley

1kg small black mussels

1½ cups (375ml) water

¼ cup (60ml) extra virgin olive oil

1   Combine breadcrumbs, garlic, rind and parsley in small bowl. Scrub mussels; remove beards.

2   Bring the water to a boil in large saucepan; add mussels. Boil, covered, about 7 minutes or until mussels open. (Discard any that do not.)

3   Preheat grill.

4   Fully open shells, discard tops. Loosen mussels from shells with a spoon; replace in shells. Place shells, in single layer, on large baking tray. Sprinkle with breadcrumb mixture; drizzle with oil. Cook under grill about 3 minutes or until browned.

SEAFOOD

octopus braised in red wine

preparation time 15 minutes cooking time 1 hour 45 minutes serves 6

⅓ cup (80ml) olive oil

600g baby onions, halved

4 cloves garlic, crushed

1.5kg cleaned baby octopus, halved

1½ cups (375ml) dry red wine

⅓ cup (95g) tomato paste

⅓ cup (80ml) red wine vinegar

3 large tomatoes (660g), peeled,
seeded, chopped coarsely

2 bay leaves

1 fresh long red chilli, chopped finely

10 drained anchovy fillets (30g),
chopped coarsely

⅓ cup finely chopped fresh oregano

1 cup coarsely chopped fresh flat-leaf parsley

1 Heat oil in large saucepan; cook onion and garlic, stirring, until onion softens. Add octopus; cook, stirring, until just changed in colour.

2 Add wine; cook, stirring, about 5 minutes or until pan liquid is reduced by about a third. Add tomato paste, vinegar, tomato, bay leaves, chilli and anchovies; bring to a boil. Reduce heat, simmer, covered, 1 hour. Uncover; simmer about 30 minutes or until sauce thickens and octopus is tender.

3 Stir in oregano and parsley off the heat; serve with thick slices of toasted ciabatta bread, if desired.

TIP Ask your fishmonger to clean the octopus and remove the beaks.

fish in garlic marinade

preparation time 10 minutes (plus marinating time) cooking time 20 minutes serves 2

2 x 250g small whole fish

1 clove garlic, crushed

½ teaspoon finely grated lemon rind

2 tablespoons lemon juice

1 tablespoon dry white wine

1 teaspoon olive oil

2 teaspoons finely chopped fresh thyme

½ teaspoon finely grated fresh ginger

½ teaspoon sugar

1   Place fish in shallow dish; pour over combined remaining ingredients. Turn fish to coat in marinade; refrigerate for several hours or overnight.
2   Preheat oven to 180°C/160°C fan-forced.
3   Remove fish from marinade; wrap in foil. Place in baking dish; bake about 20 minutes or until fish are tender. Serve with chargrilled lemon slices, if desired.

STORE Fish can be marinated a day ahead and refrigerated, covered.

fish fillets with coriander sauce

preparation time 10 minutes cooking time 25 minutes serves 2

6 x 70g white fish fillets

1 small brown onion (80g), sliced thinly

½ cup (125ml) water

¼ cup (60ml) dry vermouth

2 tablespoons lime juice

1 fresh small red chilli, chopped finely

2 tablespoons sugar

1 teaspoon cornflour

1 tablespoon finely chopped
fresh coriander

½ medium red capsicum (100g),
sliced thinly

2 green onions, cut into 5cm lengths

¼ cup firmly packed fresh
coriander leaves, extra

1   Preheat oven to 180°C/160°C fan-forced.
2   Place fish in shallow ovenproof dish; top with brown onion. Pour over combined water, vermouth and 1 tablespoon of the juice. Bake, covered, about 15 minutes or until fish is tender. Remove fish from dish; keep warm. Strain and reserve liquid.
3   Stir reserved liquid, chilli, sugar and combined cornflour and remaining juice in small saucepan over heat until sugar dissolves; bring to a boil. Reduce heat, simmer until mixture thickens. Stir in chopped coriander. Arrange fish, capsicum, green onion and coriander leaves on serving plate; drizzle with sauce.

STORE Cook recipe just before serving.

fish kebabs with chilli sauce

preparation time 15 minutes (plus refrigeration time) cooking time 15 minutes serves 2

300g tuna steaks, cut into 3cm pieces

1 tablespoon soy sauce

1 clove garlic, crushed

¼ teaspoon grated fresh ginger

1 medium red capsicum (200g),
chopped coarsely

1 medium green capsicum (200g),
chopped coarsely

2 teaspoons vegetable oil

1 cup cooked long-grain rice

CHILLI SAUCE

1 fresh small red chilli, chopped finely

2 cloves garlic, crushed

1 tablespoon finely chopped
fresh coriander

1 tablespoon fish sauce

1 tablespoon lime juice

1½ tablespoons brown sugar

1 tablespoon mirin

⅓ cup (80ml) water

1   Combine fish with sauce, garlic and ginger in large bowl. Cover; refrigerate for 1 hour.
2   Make chilli sauce.
3   Preheat grill.
4   Thread fish and capsicum alternately onto 4 skewers. Brush with oil; cook under hot grill until fish is tender. Serve kebabs on rice topped with sauce.
CHILLI SAUCE Grind chilli, garlic and coriander to a smooth paste. Add fish sauce, juice, sugar, mirin and the water. Transfer mixture to small saucepan; stir until sugar is dissolved and sauce heated through.

TIP You will need to cook about ⅓ cup (65g) long-grain rice for this recipe.
STORE Fish can be marinated a day ahead and refrigerated, covered.

swordfish with olive paste

preparation time 15 minutes cooking time 10 minutes serves 4

200g kalamata olives, seeded

¼ cup (50g) drained capers

⅓ cup finely chopped fresh dill

⅓ cup finely chopped fresh flat-leaf parsley

2 cloves garlic, crushed

2 tablespoons lemon juice

4 swordfish steaks (800g)

1 Blend or process olives, capers, dill, parsley, garlic and juice until mixture forms an almost smooth paste.

2 Cook fish on heated oiled barbecue, uncovered, until browned both sides and just cooked through. Spread olive paste over fish to serve.

TIP Olive paste can be made 3 days ahead and refrigerated, covered.

char-grilled squid, rocket and parmesan salad

preparation time 20 minutes cooking time 10 minutes serves 4

1kg squid hoods

2 tablespoons olive oil

1 tablespoon finely grated lemon rind

⅓ cup (80ml) lemon juice

1 clove garlic, crushed

150g rocket

150g semi-dried tomatoes, drained, chopped coarsely

1 small red onion (100g), sliced thinly

1 tablespoon drained baby capers, rinsed

80g parmesan cheese, shaved

2 tablespoons balsamic vinegar

2 tablespoons olive oil, extra

1 Halve squid lengthways, score insides in crosshatch pattern then cut into 5cm strips. Combine squid in medium bowl with oil, rind, juice and garlic, cover; refrigerate 10 minutes.

2 Meanwhile, combine rocket, tomato, onion, capers and cheese in large bowl.

3 Drain squid; discard marinade. Cook squid in batches, on heated oiled grill plate (or grill or barbecue) until browned and cooked through.

4 Add squid to rocket salad with combined vinegar and extra oil; toss gently to combine.

deep-fried whitebait

preparation time 10 minutes cooking time 15 minutes serves 4

1 cup (150g) plain flour

¼ cup coarsely chopped fresh basil

1 teaspoon garlic salt

500g whitebait

vegetable oil, for deep-frying

SPICED MAYONNAISE DIP

1 cup (300g) mayonnaise

2 cloves garlic, crushed

2 tablespoons lemon juice

1 tablespoon drained capers, chopped finely

1 tablespoon coarsely chopped fresh flat-leaf parsley

1 Combine flour, basil and garlic salt in large bowl. Toss whitebait in flour mixture, in batches, until coated.

2 Heat oil in medium saucepan. Deep-fry whitebait, in batches, until browned and cooked through; drain on absorbent paper.

3 Make spiced mayonnaise dip; serve with deep-fried whitebait.
   SPICED MAYONNAISE DIP Combine all ingredients in small serving bowl.

swordfish with celery and bean salad

preparation time 15 minutes cooking time 5 minutes serves 4

⅓ cup (80ml) lemon juice

2 cloves garlic, chopped finely

¼ teaspoon salt

¼ teaspoon cracked black pepper

⅓ cup (80ml) extra virgin olive oil

1 tablespoon fresh oregano leaves, torn

1 tablespoon baby capers, rinsed, drained

4 swordfish steaks (700g)

CELERY AND BEAN SALAD

2 trimmed celery stalks (200g), halved, sliced thinly

300g can cannellini beans, rinsed, drained

¼ cup coarsely chopped young celery leaves

1 Whisk juice, garlic, salt, pepper and oil in medium bowl until thickened slightly. Stir in oregano and capers.

2 Place ingredients for celery and bean salad in small bowl with half the dressing; toss gently to combine.

3 Heat lightly oiled, large frying pan; cook fish until cooked as desired. Remove from pan.

4 Add remaining dressing to same pan, bring to a boil.

5 Serve fish with celery and bean salad, drizzled with warm dressing.

TIP Swordfish can be replaced with any firm white fish.

char-grilled swordfish with roasted mediterranean vegetables

preparation time 20 minutes cooking time 25 minutes serves 4

1 medium red capsicum (200g), sliced thickly

1 medium yellow capsicum (200g), sliced thickly

1 medium eggplant (300g), sliced thickly

2 large zucchini (300g), sliced thickly

½ cup (125ml) olive oil

250g cherry tomatoes

¼ cup (60ml) balsamic vinegar

1 clove garlic, crushed

2 teaspoons sugar

4 x 220g swordfish steaks

¼ cup coarsely chopped fresh basil

1 Preheat oven to 220°C/200°C fan-forced.

2 Combine capsicums, eggplant and zucchini with 2 tablespoons of the oil in large baking dish; roast, uncovered, 15 minutes. Add tomatoes; roast, uncovered, further 5 minutes or until vegetables are just tender.

3 Meanwhile, combine remaining oil, vinegar, garlic and sugar in screw-top jar; shake well. Brush a third of the dressing over fish; cook fish, in batches, on heated oiled grill plate (or grill or barbecue) until browned both sides and cooked as desired.

4 Combine vegetables in large bowl with basil and remaining dressing; toss gently to combine. Divide vegetables among serving plates; top with fish.

spaghetti bolognese

preparation time 15 minutes cooking time 2¼ hours serves 4

2 tablespoons olive oil

1 large brown onion (200g), chopped finely

750g beef mince

425g canned tomatoes

1 teaspoon fresh basil

1 teaspoon fresh oregano

½ teaspoon fresh thyme

⅓ cup (95g) tomato paste

1 litre (4 cups) water

250g spaghetti

grated parmesan cheese

1 Heat oil in large saucepan; cook onion until golden brown. Add beef to pan; cook until beef browns, mashing with fork occasionally to break up lumps. Pour off any surplus fat.

2 Push undrained tomatoes through sieve; add to pan. Add herbs, paste and the water; bring to a boil. Reduce heat, simmer, very gently, uncovered, about 1½ hours, or until nearly all liquid evaporates. [Can be made 2 days ahead to this stage and refrigerated, covered, or frozen for up to 3 months.]

3 Cook pasta in large saucepan of boiling water, uncovered, until just tender; drain well.

4 Arrange hot pasta in individual serving bowls; top with sauce. Serve sprinkled with cheese.

TIP A true bolognese sauce contains no garlic, however 2 crushed cloves of garlic can be added to the tomatoes in step 2, if desired.

cauliflower chilli spaghetti

preparation 15 minutes cooking 15 minutes serves 4 to 6

¼ cup (60ml) extra virgin olive oil

700g small cauliflower florets

375g spaghetti

⅓ cup (50g) pine nuts, chopped

2 cloves garlic, crushed

6 drained anchovies, chopped

½ teaspoon dried chilli flakes

1 tablespoon lemon juice

¼ cup coarsely chopped fresh
flat-leaf parsley

2 tablespoons extra virgin olive oil, extra

1   Heat oil in large frying pan; cook cauliflower, stirring, about 10 minutes or until just tender and browned lightly.
2   Meanwhile, cook pasta in large saucepan of boiling water, uncovered, until just tender; drain.
3   Add pine nuts to cauliflower; cook, stirring, until browned lightly. Add garlic, anchovies and chilli; cook, stirring, until mixture is fragrant. Stir in juice and parsley.
4   Toss cauliflower mixture with spaghetti and extra oil.

TIP This recipe is best made just before serving.

rigatoni with eggplant sauce

preparation time 10 minutes cooking time 20 minutes serves 4

¼ cup (60ml) olive oil

1 medium brown onion (150g), chopped finely

2 trimmed celery stalks (200g), chopped finely

1 clove garlic, crushed

2 tablespoons brandy

1 medium eggplant (300g), sliced thinly

2⅓ cups (580ml) bottled tomato pasta sauce

½ cup (140g) tomato paste

½ cup (125ml) water

375g rigatoni

¼ cup (20g) finely grated parmesan cheese

1 Heat oil in large saucepan; cook onion, celery and garlic, stirring, until onion softens. Add brandy; cook, stirring, until brandy evaporates. Add eggplant; cook, stirring, until eggplant is tender.

2 Stir in pasta sauce, paste and the water; bring to a boil. Reduce heat, simmer, uncovered, about 10 minutes or until sauce thickens slightly. [Can be made 2 days ahead to this stage and refrigerated, covered.]

3 Meanwhile, cook pasta in large saucepan of boiling water, uncovered, until just tender; drain. Place pasta in large warmed bowl with half of the eggplant sauce; toss gently to combine. Divide pasta among serving plates; top each with remaining sauce. Serve with cheese.

TIP Before serving, warm large bowls and platters, by placing in a sink of very hot water 10 minutes; dry before using.

herbed ricotta ravioli in tomato broth

preparation time 20 minutes (plus refrigeration time) cooking time 10 minutes serves 4

⅓ cup (30g) finely grated parmesan cheese

⅔ cup (130g) low-fat ricotta cheese

1 tablespoon finely chopped fresh basil

2 tablespoons finely chopped fresh chives

24 wonton wrappers

16 medium egg tomatoes (1.2kg)

2 green onions, sliced thinly

1 Combine cheeses and herbs in small bowl. Place one rounded teaspoon of cheese mixture in centre of each of 12 wonton wrappers; brush around edge with a little water. Top each with a remaining wrapper, press around edges firmly to seal. Place ravioli on tray, cover; refrigerate 20 minutes.

2 Meanwhile, bring large saucepan of water to a boil. Place cored tomatoes in pan; return to a boil. Cook, uncovered, 2 minutes. Strain tomatoes over large bowl; reserve cooking liquid.

3 Blend or process tomatoes, in batches, until smooth; push through a food mill (mouli) or sieve into small saucepan; bring to a boil. Reduce heat, simmer broth, uncovered, 5 minutes.

4 Meanwhile, cook ravioli in large saucepan of reserved cooking liquid, uncovered, about 4 minutes or until ravioli float to the surface; discard cooking liquid. Divide tomato broth and ravioli among serving bowls; sprinkle with onion.

spaghetti with rocket, pine nuts and sun-dried capsicum

preparation time 10 minutes cooking time 15 minutes serves 4

500g spaghettini

270g jar sun-dried capsicums

¼ cup (60ml) olive oil

½ cup (80g) toasted pine nuts, chopped coarsely

2 fresh small red thai chillies, chopped finely

2 cloves garlic, crushed

100g rocket, shredded finely

⅓ cup (25g) coarsely grated parmesan cheese

1 Cook pasta in large saucepan of boiling water, uncovered, until just tender; drain.

2 Meanwhile, drain capsicums over small bowl; reserve ¼ cup of the oil. Coarsely chop ½ cup of the capsicum; return remaining capsicum and oil to jar, keep for another use.

3 Heat reserved oil with olive oil in large saucepan; cook pine nuts, chilli and garlic, stirring, until fragrant. Add pasta, chopped capsicum and rocket; toss until rocket is just wilted.

4 Serve pasta sprinkled with cheese.

spaghetti with herbed ricotta

preparation time 10 minutes cooking time 15 minutes serves 4

500g spaghetti

450g fresh ricotta cheese

3 egg yolks

¾ cup (180ml) milk

⅓ cup coarsely chopped fresh
flat-leaf parsley

¼ cup coarsely chopped fresh basil

3 green onions, chopped finely

2 cloves garlic, crushed

¼ cup (20g) finely grated pepato cheese

1 Cook pasta in large saucepan of boiling water, uncovered, until just tender; drain.

2 Whisk ricotta, yolks and milk in large bowl until smooth; stir in herbs, onion, garlic and pepato cheese.

3 Add pasta to ricotta mixture; toss gently to combine. Sprinkle with freshly ground black pepper to serve, if desired.

TIPS Pepato can be substituted with another hard cheese, such as romano or an aged provolone.
You can use other herbs, such as chives or oregano, instead of the basil, if you prefer.

ricotta and spinach stuffed pasta shells

preparation time 20 minutes cooking time 1 hour 5 minutes serves 4

32 large pasta shells (280g)

500g spinach

250g low-fat ricotta cheese

500g low-fat cottage cheese

600ml bottled tomato pasta sauce

1 cup (250ml) vegetable stock

1 tablespoon finely grated parmesan cheese

1 Cook pasta in large saucepan of boiling water, uncovered, 3 minutes; drain. Cool slightly.

2 Preheat oven to 180°C/160°C fan-forced. Oil shallow 2-litre (8 cup) ovenproof dish.

3 Boil, steam or microwave spinach until just wilted; drain. Chop spinach finely; squeeze out excess liquid.

4 Combine spinach in large bowl with ricotta and cottage cheese; spoon spinach mixture into pasta shells.

5 Combine sauce and stock in dish. Place pasta shells in dish; sprinkle with parmesan. Bake, covered, about 1 hour or until pasta is tender.

pasta with tomatoes, artichokes and olives

preparation time 30 minutes cooking time 30 minutes serves 4

2 teaspoons olive oil

1 medium brown onion (150g), chopped finely

2 cloves garlic, crushed

¼ cup (60ml) dry white wine

2 x 425g cans tomatoes

2 tablespoons tomato paste

½ teaspoon sugar

½ cup (80g) seeded black olives

390g can artichoke hearts, drained, quartered

2 tablespoons finely sliced fresh basil

375g spiral pasta

⅓ cup (25g) flaked parmesan cheese

1 Heat oil in large saucepan; cook onion and garlic, stirring, until onion softens. Add wine, undrained crushed tomatoes, paste and sugar; simmer, uncovered, about 15 minutes or until sauce thickens. Add olives, artichoke and basil; stir until hot.

2 Meanwhile, cook pasta in large saucepan of boiling water, uncovered, until just tender; drain.

3 Place pasta with half of the sauce in large bowl; toss well to combine. Serve pasta topped with remaining sauce and cheese.

There are many versions of this popular dish, but an authentic Salade niçoise (originally from the Provençal city of Nice) always includes ingredients that speak of this sun-kissed region of France: tomatoes, capers, olives and garlic. A typical recipe also includes tuna, anchovies, egg and raw vegetables.

TIP Niçoise olives, tiny ovate brown-black olives with a rich nutty flavour, are grown all over the rough, hilly terrain of Provence. If unavailable, substitute any small brown olive.

salade niçoise

preparation time 1 hour **cooking time** 5 minutes **serves** 4

1 medium red onion (170g)

4 medium egg tomatoes (300g)

3 trimmed celery stalks (300g)

3 hard-boiled eggs

200g green beans

12 whole canned anchovy fillets, drained, halved lengthways

425g can tuna in oil, drained, flaked

100g niçoise olives

2 tablespoons baby capers

2 tablespoons shredded fresh basil

LEMON GARLIC DRESSING

½ cup (125ml) extra virgin olive oil

¼ cup (60ml) lemon juice

1 clove garlic, crushed

1 teaspoon sugar

1 Quarter onion lengthways; slice thinly. Cut tomatoes into wedges; remove seeds. Slice celery thinly. Shell and quarter eggs.

2 Top and tail beans; boil, steam or microwave beans until just tender, drain. Rinse beans under cold water; drain well.

3 Make lemon garlic dressing.

4 Layer onion, tomato, celery, egg, beans, anchovy and tuna on serving plate. Sprinkle with olives, capers and basil; drizzle with lemon garlic dressing. **LEMON GARLIC DRESSING** Place ingredients in screw-top jar; shake well.

SERVING SUGGESTION This salad can be served on its own as a light meal, accompanied by warm crusty bread and a glass of red wine. As a first course, it goes well with barbecued fish or other grilled seafood.

SALADS

Guacamole is an avocado salad, sometimes used as an accompaniment but best eaten on its own with corn chips. For extra flavour, try adding either crushed garlic, chopped green onion, finely chopped chilli or a few drops of Tabasco sauce.

guacamole

preparation time 20 minutes **makes** 3¼ cups (760g)

1 medium white onion (150g)

2 small tomatoes (260g)

2 medium avocados (500g)

1 tablespoon lime juice

2 tablespoons coarsely chopped fresh coriander

1 Chop onion and tomatoes finely.

2 Using a fork, mash avocados in medium bowl until almost smooth. Add onion, tomato, juice and coriander; mix well.

SERVING SUGGESTION serve guacamole with corn chips, salsa and sour cream. Also good with tacos, nachos and other Mexican dishes.

caprese salad

preparation time 15 minutes **serves** 4

3 large egg tomatoes (270g), sliced thinly

5 bocconcini cheese (300g), sliced thinly

2 tablespoons olive oil

⅓ cup loosely packed fresh basil leaves

1 Arrange tomato and cheese alternately on serving platter.

2 Drizzle with oil; sprinkle with basil, and salt and pepper, if desired.

CAPRESE SALAD

white bean salad

preparation time 20 minutes serves 4

2 x 400g cans white beans, rinsed, drained

1 medium red onion (170g), chopped finely

⅔ cup (100g) drained semi-dried tomatoes

150g mozzarella cheese, cut into 1cm pieces

½ cup (75g) seeded kalamata olives

150g rocket

OREGANO BALSAMIC VINAIGRETTE

1 clove garlic, crushed

1 tablespoon finely chopped fresh oregano

¼ cup (60ml) balsamic vinegar

¼ cup (60ml) extra virgin olive oil

1   Combine beans, onion, tomato, cheese and olives in medium bowl.
2   Make oregano balsamic vinaigrette.
3   Drizzle salad with vinaigrette; toss gently to combine. Serve with rocket.
    OREGANO BALSAMIC VINAIGRETTE Place ingredients in screw-top jar; shake well.

TIP Many varieties of already cooked white beans are available canned, among them cannellini, butter and haricot beans; any of these are suitable for use in this salad.

You can make these creamy salads by whisking them in a bowl or, for a smoother texture, you can use an electric blender or processor. Serve them as a first course with wedges of ciabatta, lavash, naan, pide, pitta or pocket pitta.

Tahini, a paste made from sesame seeds, is available from selected supermarkets and delicatessens.

tahini salad

preparation time 10 minutes **makes** 1½ cups (350g)

¾ cup (180ml) tahini

2 cloves garlic, crushed

¼ cup (60ml) lemon juice

¼ cup (60ml) water

¼ teaspoon ground cumin

1 tablespoon finely chopped fresh flat-leaf parsley

1 Combine tahini and garlic in small bowl.

2 Gradually beat in juice, water, cumin and parsley, beating well until mixture thickens.

SERVING SUGGESTION This Middle-Eastern cream salad is popular as a first course with Turkish bread or as an accompaniment to both hot and cold main dishes. Try it with sliced, toasted Turkish bread.

Taramasalata is a "mayonnaise" made with tarama, the dried, salt-pressed and lightly smoked roe of the grey mullet. As this can be expensive, smoked cod's roe can be used instead. If you use genuine tarama you'll get an orange-coloured taramasalata, whereas with smoked cod's roe it is more rosy pink in colour. Taramasalata can be made a week ahead; keep, covered, in refrigerator.

taramasalata

preparation time 10 minutes **makes** about 2 cups (670g)

4 slices stale white bread

100g can tarama

1 small brown onion (80g), chopped coarsely

1 clove garlic, quartered

¼ cup (60ml) lemon juice

1½ cups (375ml) olive oil

1 Discard crusts from bread; soak bread in cold water for 2 minutes. Drain; squeeze water from bread with hands.
2 Blend or process bread, tarama, onion, garlic and juice until combined. With motor operating, add oil in thin stream; process until mixture thickens.

SERVING SUGGESTION Serve as a dip, with wedges of ciabatta or Turkish bread and vegetable sticks.

cheese-filled zucchini flowers
with tomato basil sauce

preparation time 40 minutes cooking time 20 minutes serves 4

200g green peppercorn cream cheese, softened

1 tablespoon finely chopped fresh chives

¼ cup (15g) fresh breadcrumbs

16 baby zucchini with flowers attached (320g)

2 tablespoons olive oil

TOMATO BASIL SAUCE

1 tablespoon olive oil

1 small brown onion (80g), chopped finely

1 clove garlic, crushed

400g can diced tomatoes

1 tablespoon finely shredded fresh basil

1 Combine cheese, chives and breadcrumbs in small bowl. Discard stamens from zucchini flowers; fill flowers with cheese mixture, twist petal tops to enclose filling.

2 Make tomato basil sauce.

3 Meanwhile, heat oil in large frying pan; cook zucchini flowers, covered, about 5 minutes or until baby zucchini are tender, turning occasionally.

4 Remove zucchini carefully from dish to serving plates; serve with sauce.
TOMATO BASIL SAUCE Heat oil in medium frying pan; cook onion and garlic, stirring, until onion softens. Stir in undrained tomatoes; bring to a boil. Reduce heat, simmer, uncovered, about 20 minutes or until sauce thickens. Remove from heat; stir in basil.

TIP Substitute any soft cheese, such as ricotta or neufchâtel, for the green peppercorn cheese, if you prefer.

VEGETABLES

vegetable moussaka

preparation time 10 minutes cooking time 50 minutes (plus cooling time) serves 2

1 large eggplant (500g), sliced thickly

2 large tomatoes (500g), chopped finely

1 teaspoon sugar

2 teaspoons margarine

1 tablespoon plain flour

1 cup (250ml) skim milk

2 tablespoons finely grated parmesan cheese

2 tablespoons finely chopped fresh basil

1   Preheat oven to 200°C/180°C fan-forced.

2   Place eggplant in single layer on oven tray; bake, uncovered, 15 minutes. Turn; bake another 15 minutes or until browned lightly. Cool 10 minutes.

3   Cook tomato and sugar in small saucepan, stirring occasionally, for about 30 minutes or until tomato is soft and liquid almost evaporated.

4   Meanwhile, melt margarine in small saucepan, add flour; cook, stirring, 1 minute. Gradually add milk; stir over medium heat until sauce boils and thickens. Stir in half of the cheese and half of the basil. Stir remaining basil through tomato mixture.

5   Spread one-third of tomato mixture, eggplant and cheese sauce in two ovenproof dishes (2-cup capacity); repeat with two more layers. Sprinkle with remaining cheese. Bake, uncovered, about 15 minutes or until browned lightly.

TIP Moussaka can be prepared 3 hours ahead and refrigerated, covered.

WARM ZUCCHINI SALAD WITH GARLIC CRUMBS

cucumber, yogurt and mint salad

preparation time 10 minutes (plus standing time) **makes** 4½ cups (940g)

3 large green cucumbers (1.2kg)

2 teaspoons coarse cooking salt

¾ cup (180ml) yogurt

1 tablespoon finely chopped fresh mint

1 clove garlic, crushed

1 Seed cucumbers; chop finely.

2 Place cucumber in colander, sprinkle with salt; stand 15 minutes. Rinse under cold water; drain on absorbent paper.

3 Combine cucumber in medium bowl with yogurt, mint and garlic.

SERVING SUGGESTION Serve this refreshing accompaniment to any hot, spicy dish – particularly Indian curries – or serve it with crisp pappadums as a starter.

warm zucchini salad with garlic crumbs

preparation time 15 minutes **cooking time** 15 minutes **serves** 8

2 tablespoons extra virgin olive oil

40g butter

2 thick slices ciabatta (50g), crusts removed, chopped finely in cubes

2 cloves garlic, crushed

1 tablespoon toasted pine nuts, chopped coarsely

1 teaspoon finely grated lemon rind

2 tablespoons chopped fresh flat-leaf parsley

1 tablespoon dried currants

24 small zucchini flowers (700g)

1 Heat half of the oil and half of the butter in large frying pan; cook bread, stirring, until browned lightly. Add garlic; cook until fragrant. Stir in pine nuts, rind, parsley and currants. Remove from pan; cover to keep warm.

2 Heat remaining oil and remaining butter in same frying pa; cook zucchini, covered loosely, until browned lightly and just tender.

3 Serve zucchini sprinkled with bread mixture.

TIP If zucchini flowers are not available, substitute small zucchini quartered lengthways.

capsicums stuffed with pilaf

preparation time 20 minutes cooking time 55 minutes serves 4

2 teaspoons olive oil

1 medium red onion (170g), chopped finely

1 tablespoon slivered almonds

²⁄₃ cup (130g) white long-grain rice

1 cup (250ml) water

2 tablespoons finely chopped dried apricots

¼ cup (35g) sun-dried tomatoes,
chopped finely

¼ cup finely chopped fresh flat-leaf parsley

4 medium red capsicums (800g)

cooking-oil spray

ROASTED TOMATO SALAD

2 medium tomatoes (300g),
cut into thick wedges

1 tablespoon apple cider vinegar

½ teaspoon cracked black pepper

1 teaspoon white sugar

1 cup firmly packed fresh flat-leaf parsley

½ cup firmly packed fresh mint

1 Preheat oven to 200°C/180°C fan-forced.
2 Heat oil in medium saucepan; cook onion and nuts, stirring, until onion softens. Add rice; cook, stirring, 1 minute. Add the water; bring to a boil. Reduce heat, simmer, covered, about 15 minutes or until liquid is absorbed and rice is just tender. Stir in apricot, tomato and parsley.
3 Carefully cut tops off capsicums; discard tops. Discard seeds and membranes, leaving capsicum intact. Divide pilaf among capsicums; place capsicums on oven tray, spray with oil. Roast, uncovered, on oven tray 10 minutes. Cover loosely with foil; cook about 20 minutes or until capsicums are just soft.
4 Meanwhile, make roasted tomato salad.
5 Serve capsicums with roasted tomato salad.
   ROASTED TOMATO SALAD Combine tomato with vinegar, pepper and sugar in medium bowl. Drain; reserve liquid. Place tomato on oven tray; roast, uncovered, alongside capsicums about 10 minutes or until tomato just softens. Place tomato and reserved liquid in medium bowl with herbs; toss gently.

spicy bean casserole

preparation time 10 minutes (plus standing time) cooking time 1 hour serves 2

½ cup (100g) dried red kidney beans

½ cup (100g) dried chick peas

2 teaspoons margarine

1 medium red onion (170g), sliced thinly

1 medium carrot (120g), chopped coarsely

1 small red capsicum (150g), chopped finely

1 clove garlic, crushed

1 fresh small red chilli, chopped finely

1 teaspoon ground cumin

½ teaspoon ground cinnamon

½ teaspoon ground nutmeg

410g can tomatoes

½ cup (125ml) vegetable stock

2 teaspoons tomato paste

½ cup (100g) canned corn kernels, drained

2 teaspoons finely chopped
fresh flat-leaf parsley

1 Cover beans and chick peas with water in small bowl. Stand overnight; drain.

2 Heat margarine in large saucepan; cook onion, carrot, capsicum, garlic and chilli until onion is soft. Stir in cumin, cinnamon and nutmeg; cook 1 minute.

3 Stir in beans and chick peas, undrained crushed tomatoes, stock and paste; bring to a boil. Reduce heat, simmer, covered, for about 45 minutes, stirring occasionally, or until beans and chick peas are tender. Stir in corn; simmer further 5 minutes.

4 Sprinkle with parsley just before serving.

TIP Recipe can be made a day ahead and refrigerated, covered.

artichokes with lemon caper dressing

preparation time 20 minutes cooking time 45 minutes serves 4

4 medium artichokes (800g)

½ cup (125ml) lemon juice

½ cup (125ml) light olive oil

2 cloves garlic, crushed

2 tablespoons capers, chopped coarsely

¼ cup coarsely chopped fresh flat-leaf parsley

1 Trim artichoke stalks to 1cm; remove tough outer leaves. Cut off top quarter of remaining leaves. Using small spoon, scoop out centre of artichoke to remove choke; discard.

2 Place artichokes, cut-side down, in steamer. Steam artichokes, covered tightly, about 45 minutes or until stems are tender when tested with a skewer; cut in half.

3 Place hot artichokes on serving plates; drizzle with combined remaining ingredients to serve.

garlicky beans with pine nuts

preparation time 30 minutes cooking time 15 minutes serves 4

400g baby beans, trimmed

¼ cup (60ml) olive oil

1 clove garlic, sliced thinly

2 tablespoons toasted pine nuts, chopped

1 Boil, steam or microwave beans until just tender; drain. Add beans to large bowl of iced water; drain well. Place in large bowl.

2 Heat oil and garlic in small frying pan over low heat until garlic just changes colour. Add nuts; stir until heated through.

3 Drizzle nut mixture over beans.

   TIPS The beans can be served hot or cold. This recipe can be prepared several hours ahead. Add pine nut mixture close to serving.

97

tomato

preparation time 10 minutes cooking time 40 minutes
(plus cooling time) makes 3½ cups

1 tablespoon olive oil

1 large brown onion (200g), chopped coarsely

2 tablespoons brown sugar

3 x 400g cans diced tomatoes

¼ teaspoon ground allspice

½ teaspoon celery salt

2 tablespoons tomato paste

⅓ cup (80ml) white vinegar

1 Heat oil in large saucepan; cook onion, stirring, until soft. Add
   sugar, undrained tomatoes, allspice and celery salt; bring to
   a boil. Reduce heat, simmer, uncovered, stirring occasionally,
   about 30 minutes or until mixture thickens. Stir in paste and
   vinegar; cook, uncovered, 5 minutes.

2 Blend or process sauce until smooth; push through fine sieve
   into medium bowl. Discard solids. Serve sauce cold.

tangy barbecue

preparation time 5 minutes
cooking time 25 minutes makes 2 cups

1 cup (250ml) tomato sauce

½ cup (125ml) apple cider vinegar

¼ cup (60ml) worcestershire sauce

⅔ cup (150g) firmly packed brown sugar

2 tablespoons american-style mustard

1 fresh small red thai chilli, chopped finely

1 clove garlic, crushed

1 tablespoon lemon juice

1 Combine ingredients in medium saucepan; bring to a boil.
   Reduce heat, simmer, uncovered, stirring occasionally,
   20 minutes.

SAUCES

TOMATO

TANGY BARBECUE

green goddess

preparation time 10 minutes makes 1 cup

1 cup (300g) mayonnaise

2 anchovy fillets, drained, chopped finely

2 green onions, sliced thinly

2 teaspoons finely chopped fresh flat-leaf parsley

2 teaspoons finely chopped fresh chives

2 teaspoons finely chopped fresh tarragon

2 teaspoons cider vinegar

1 Combine ingredients in small bowl.

béchamel

preparation time 5 minutes
cooking time 15 minutes makes 1 cup

30g butter

2 tablespoons plain flour

1¼ cups (310ml) hot milk

pinch nutmeg

1 Melt butter in medium saucepan, add flour; cook, stirring, until mixture bubbles and thickens.

2 Gradually add milk, stirring, until mixture boils and thickens. Stir in nutmeg.

mornay

preparation time 5 minutes
cooking time 5 minutes makes 2 cups

1 cup (250ml) béchamel sauce (see recipe above)

¼ cup (60ml) cream

1 egg yolk

1 cup (120g) coarsely grated emmentaler cheese

1 Bring béchamel to a boil in medium saucepan; add cream and egg yolk, whisk 1 minute.

2 Remove pan from heat, add cheese; stir until cheese melts.

TIP Substitute gruyère or cheddar for emmentaler.

mild curry

preparation time 5 minutes cooking time 15 minutes
makes about 1 litre (4 cups)

15g butter

1 small onion (80g), chopped

1 trimmed stalk celery (100g), chopped

1 clove garlic, crushed

1½ tablespoons plain flour

1 teaspoon sugar

½ teaspoon curry powder

1½ cups (375ml) fish stock

¼ teaspoon sambal oelek

2 medium tomatoes (260g), peeled, chopped

1 tablespoon tomato paste

½ small red capsicum (75g), chopped

½ small green capsicum (75g), chopped

1½ cups (125g) frozen green peas

1 tablespoon chopped fresh coriander

1 Heat butter in small saucepan; cook onion, celery and garlic, stirring, until onion is soft. Add flour, sugar and curry powder; cook, stirring, until well combined.

2 Stir in stock and sambal oelek, simmer, uncovered, about 2 minutes or until vegetables are tender; sti in coriander.

TIP Recipe can be made a day ahead.

GREEN GODDESS

BECHAMEL

rosewater baklava

preparation time 25 minutes cooking time 45 minutes makes 16

1 cup (160g) blanched almonds

1 cup (140g) pistachios

2 teaspoons ground cinnamon

1 teaspoon ground clove

1 teaspoon ground nutmeg

18 sheets filo pastry

80g butter, melted

ROSEWATER SYRUP

1 cup (250ml) water

¼ cup (90g) honey

1 teaspoon rosewater

1 Preheat oven to 180°C/160°C fan-forced. Grease deep 23cm-square cake pan.

2 Process nuts and spices until chopped finely; spread nut mixture onto oven tray. Roast about 10 minutes or until browned lightly.

3 Increase oven temperature to 200°C/180°C fan-forced.

4 Cut pastry sheets to fit base of pan. Layer three pastry squares, brushing each with butter; place in pan, sprinkle with ⅓ cup of the nut mixture. Repeat layering with remaining pastry, butter and nut mixture, ending with pastry.

5 Using sharp knife, cut baklava into quarters; cut each quarter into a triangle then cut each triangle in half. Bake 25 minutes.

6 Reduce oven temperature to 150°C/130°C fan-forced; bake baklava further 10 minutes.

7 Meanwhile, make rosewater syrup. Pour hot syrup over hot baklava; cool in pan.

ROSEWATER SYRUP Stir ingredients in small saucepan over heat, without boiling, until sugar dissolves; bring to a boil. Reduce heat, simmer, uncovered, without stirring, about 5 minutes or until thickened slightly.

SWEETS

zabaglione

preparation time 5 minutes cooking time 15 minutes serves 6

2 eggs

4 egg yolks

½ cup (110g) caster sugar

⅓ cup (80ml) marsala

12 savoiardi sponge finger biscuits

1 Place eggs, yolks and sugar in large heatproof bowl over pan of simmering water, ensuring the water does not touch bottom of bowl.

2 Beat egg mixture constantly with electric mixer or hand whisk until light and fluffy. Gradually add marsala while continuing to beat 10 minutes or until mixture is thick and creamy.

3 Spoon zabaglione into small serving glasses; serve with sponge fingers.

almond macaroons

preparation time 20 minutes cooking time 10 minutes (plus cooling time) makes 22

1 cup (125g) almond meal

½ cup (110g) caster sugar

1 drop almond essence

1 egg white

¼ cup (40g) blanched almonds

icing sugar, for dusting

1 Preheat oven to 160°C/140°C fan-forced. Line oven trays with baking paper.

2 Combine almond meal and sugar in medium bowl. Stir in combined essence and egg white; mix well.

3 Roll two level teaspoons of mixture into balls, place 3cm apart on trays. Place one almond on top of each macaroon and flatten slightly.

4 Bake about 10 minutes or until browned lightly. Stand on trays 5 minutes before transferring to wire rack to cool. Dust lightly with sifted icing sugar.

STORE Keep biscuits in an airtight container for up to 3 weeks. Suitable to freeze for up to 3 months.

SWEETS

105

chocolate cannoli

preparation time 1 hour (plus refrigeration time) **cooking time** 25 minutes **serves** 8

1½ cups (225g) plain flour

2 tablespoons cocoa powder

2 egg yolks

1 egg, beaten lightly

2 tablespoons coffee-flavoured liqueur

1 tablespoon olive oil

1½ tablespoons water, approximately

plain flour, extra

1 egg white

vegetable oil for deep-frying

16 strawberries

RICOTTA FILLING

1kg ricotta cheese

½ cup (80g) icing sugar

1⅓ cups (200g) white chocolate melts, melted

⅓ cup (80ml) coffee-flavoured liqueur

CHOCOLATE SAUCE

⅔ cup (160ml) cream

100g dark eating chocolate, chopped coarsely

1 Process flour, cocoa, yolks, egg, liqueur and olive oil with enough of the water to form a soft dough; process until mixture forms a ball. Knead dough on floured surface about 5 minutes or until smooth. Wrap in plastic wrap; refrigerate 1 hour.

2 Meanwhile, make ricotta filling.

3 Divide dough into two portions. Roll each portion through pasta machine set on thickest setting. Fold dough in half; roll through machine, dusting with a little extra flour when necessary. Keep rolling dough through machine, adjusting setting so dough becomes thinner with each roll. Roll to second thinnest setting. Cut dough into 24 x 9cm-squares. Ensure each piece is 5mm short of the ends of the pieces of pasta or metal moulds.

4 Place whichever mould (see tip) you're using on end of each square.

5 Roll dough around mould; brush overlapping end with a little egg white. Make sure egg white does not touch the mould; press firmly to seal. Repeat with remaining squares.

6 Heat vegetable oil in large saucepan. Deep-fry cannoli, in batches, until crisp; drain on absorbent paper. Carefully remove warm cannoli shells from moulds; cool. [Can be made a day ahead to this stage and stored in airtight container.]

7 Spoon ricotta filling into large piping bag fitted with plain 1cm tube; pipe ricotta filling into cannoli.

8 Make chocolate sauce.

9 Serve cannoli with sauce and strawberries.

RICOTTA FILLING Beat cheese and icing sugar in large bowl with electric mixer until smooth; beat in cooled chocolate and liqueur. [Can be made a day ahead and refrigerated, covered.]

CHOCOLATE SAUCE Stir cream and chocolate in small saucepan, over low heat, until chocolate melts.

tiramisu

preparation time 25 minutes (plus refrigeration time) **serves** 6

2 tablespoons ground espresso coffee

1 cup (250ml) boiling water

½ cup (125ml) marsala

250g packet savoiardi sponge finger biscuits

300ml thickened cream

¼ cup (40g) icing sugar

2 cups (500g) mascarpone cheese

2 tablespoons marsala, extra

50g dark eating chocolate, grated coarsely

1 Combine coffee and the boiling water in coffee plunger; stand 2 minutes before plunging. Combine coffee mixture and marsala in medium heatproof bowl; cool 10 minutes.

2 Place a third of the biscuits, in single layer, over base of deep 2-litre (8-cup) dish; drizzle with a third of the coffee mixture.

3 Beat cream and sugar in small bowl until soft peaks form; transfer to large bowl. Fold in combined cheese and extra marsala.

4 Spread a third of the cream mixture over biscuits in dish. Submerge half of the remaining biscuits, one at a time, in coffee mixture, taking care the biscuits do not become so soggy that they fall apart; place over cream layer. Top biscuit layer with half of the remaining cream mixture. Repeat process with remaining biscuits, coffee mixture and cream mixture; sprinkle with chocolate. Cover; refrigerate 3 hours or overnight.

caramelised figs with spiced yogurt

preparation time 10 minutes cooking time 10 minutes **serves** 4

1 cup (280g) low-fat yogurt

¼ cup (35g) toasted pistachios, chopped coarsely

¼ teaspoon ground nutmeg

1 tablespoon caster sugar

6 large fresh figs (480g)

1 tablespoon honey

1 Combine yogurt, nuts, nutmeg and sugar in small bowl.

2 Halve figs lengthways. Brush cut-side of figs with honey.

3 Cook figs, cut-side down, uncovered, in heated large frying pan 5 minutes. Turn figs; cook, uncovered, 5 minutes or until browned lightly.

4 Serve figs with spiced yogurt.

TIP Glacé fruit salad is available from specialty food stores and some cheese counters. If unavailable, substitute glacé peaches, apricots or oranges.

ricotta cheesecake

preparation time 30 minutes (plus refrigeration and cooling time) **cooking time** 1¼ hours **serves** about 16

90g butter, softened

¼ cup (55g) caster sugar

1 egg, beaten lightly

1¼ cups (185g) plain flour

¼ cup (35g) self-raising flour

1kg ricotta cheese

1 cup (220g) caster sugar, extra

5 eggs, beaten lightly, extra

1 tablespoon finely grated lemon rind

¼ cup (60ml) lemon juice

1 teaspoon vanilla extract

¼ cup (40g) sultanas

¼ cup (80g) finely chopped glacé fruit salad

icing sugar, for dusting

1   Beat butter in bowl with an electric mixer until smooth but not changed in colour. Add caster sugar and egg; beat until just combined.

2   Stir in half of the sifted flours with a wooden spoon; work remaining flour in with hands. Knead pastry gently on floured surface until smooth. Wrap in plastic; refrigerate 30 minutes.

3   Grease a 28cm springform tin.

4   Roll pastry between sheets of floured baking paper until large enough to line base of tin. Place pastry in tin, press into base. Lightly prick with a fork, refrigerate 30 minutes.

5   Preheat oven to 200°C/180°C fan-forced.

6   Cover pastry with baking paper, fill with beans or rice; bake 10 minutes. Remove paper and beans, bake a further 15 minutes or until browned lightly; cool.

7   Reduce oven temperature to 160°C/140°C fan-forced.

8   Blend or process ricotta, extra caster sugar, extra eggs, rind, juice and extract until smooth. Transfer mixture to large bowl; gently fold in sultanas and glacé fruit salad. Pour ricotta mixture over pastry base.

9   Bake about 50 minutes or until filling is set; cool. Refrigerate 2 hours or until completely cooled. Serve dusted with sifted icing sugar.

bread and butter pudding

preparation time 20 minutes cooking time 50 minutes serves 6

6 slices white bread (270g)

40g butter, softened

½ cup (80g) sultanas

¼ teaspoon ground nutmeg

CUSTARD

1½ cups (375ml) milk

2 cups (500ml) cream

⅓ cup (75g) caster sugar

1 teaspoon vanilla extract

4 eggs

1 Preheat oven to 160°C/140°C fan-forced. Grease shallow 2-litre (8-cup) ovenproof dish.

2 Make custard.

3 Trim crusts from bread. Spread each slice with butter; cut into 4 triangles. Layer bread, overlapping slightly, in dish; sprinkle with sultanas. Pour custard over bread; sprinkle with nutmeg.

4 Place dish in large baking dish; add enough boiling water to come halfway up sides of dish. Bake about 45 minutes or until pudding sets. Remove pudding from baking dish; stand 5 minutes before serving.
   CUSTARD Combine milk, cream, sugar and extract in small saucepan; bring to a boil. Whisk eggs in large jug; whisking constantly, gradually add hot milk mixture to egg mixture.

STORE Keep in airtight container, refrigerated, for up to 2 days.

figs in honey and port

preparation time 25 minutes cooking time 25 minutes serves 4 to 6

1 medium lemon (140g)

¼ cup (60ml) port

1½ cups (375ml) water

½ cup (125g) honey

2 cinnamon sticks

1 vanilla bean, split

6 black peppercorns

8 medium fresh figs (500g)

2 medium pears (400g), quartered

HONEYED MASCARPONE

2 egg yolks

2 tablespoons honey

250g mascarpone cheese

½ teaspoon ground nutmeg

1 Peel rind thinly from lemon using a vegetable peeler. Cut any white pith from rind. Cut rind into very thin strips.

2 Combine rind, port, water, honey, cinnamon sticks, vanilla bean and peppercorns in saucepan; boil, uncovered, about 10 minutes or until reduced by half.

3 Add figs and pears to pan, simmer, uncovered, about 5 minutes or until fruit is just tender. Remove fruit to bowl.

4 Simmer syrup about 10 minutes or until thickened; pour over fruit.

5 Make honeyed mascarpone.

6 Serve fruit mixture at room temperature with honeyed mascarpone.
   HONEYED MASCARPONE Beat egg yolks and honey in small bowl with electric mixer until thick and pale. Stir in mascarpone and nutmeg.

TIP We used corella pears in this recipe.

113

ALLSPICE also known as pimento or jamaican pepper; available whole or ground. Tastes like a blend of cinnamon, clove and nutmeg.

ALMONDS flat, pointy-tipped nuts having a pitted brown shell enclosing a creamy white kernel that is covered by a brown skin.
blanched skins removed.
slivered small pieces cut lengthways.

ARTICHOKE
globe large flower-bud of a member of the thistle family; it has tough leaves and is edible in part when cooked.
hearts tender centre of the globe artichoke; available fresh from the plant or preserved, canned, in brine.

BACON RASHERS also known as bacon slices; made from cured and smoked pork side.

BARLEY, PEARL has had the husk removed then been hulled and polished so that only the"pearl" of the original grain remains, much the same as white rice.

BEANS
butter also known as lima beans; large, flat, kidney-shaped bean, off-white in colour, with a mealy texture and mild taste. Available both canned and dried.
cannellini small white bean similar in appearance and flavour to other *phaseolus vulgaris* varieties (great northern, navy or haricot). Available dried or canned.
kidney medium-size red bean, slightly floury in texture yet sweet in flavour; sold dried or canned, it's found in bean mixes and is the bean used in chilli con carne.
white in this book, some recipes may simply call for"white beans", a generic term we use for canned or dried cannellini, haricot, navy or great northern beans which are all of the same family, *phaseolus vulgaris*.

BICARBONATE OF SODA also known as baking soda; used as a leavening agent.

BREADCRUMBS
fresh bread, usually white, processed into crumbs; good for poultry stuffings and as a thickening agent.
packaged fine-textured, crunchy, purchased, white breadcrumbs.
stale 1- or 2-day-old bread made into crumbs by grating, blending or processing.

BUTTER use salted or unsalted ("sweet") butter; 125g is equal to 1 stick butter.

BUTTON MUSHROOMS small, cultivated white mushrooms having a delicate, subtle flavour. When a recipe in this book calls for an unspecified type of mushroom, use button.

CAPERS grey-green buds of a warm climate (usually mediterranean) shrub, sold either dried and salted or pickled in a vinegar brine.

CAPSICUM also known as bell pepper or, simply, pepper. Can be red, green, yellow, orange or purplish black. Discard seeds and membranes before use.

CARDAMOM can be purchased in pod, seed or ground form. Has a distinctive aromatic, sweetly rich flavour, and is one of the world's most expensive spices.

CHEESE
bocconcini baby mozzarella; from the diminutive of boccone meaning mouthful. A walnut-sized, delicate, semi-soft white cheese traditionally made from buffalo milk. Spoils rapidly so must be kept under refrigeration, in brine, for 1 or 2 days at most.
fetta a crumbly textured goat- or sheep-milk cheese having a sharp, salty taste. Ripened and stored in salted whey.
gruyère a hard-rind Swiss cheese with small holes and a nutty, slightly salty flavour. A popular cheese for soufflés.
haloumi a firm, creamed-coloured sheep-milk cheese matured in brine; tastes like a minty, salty fetta in flavour. Haloumi can be grilled or fried, briefly, without breaking down.
mascarpone an Italian fresh cultured-cream product made in much the same way as yogurt. Whiteish to creamy yellow in colour, with a buttery-rich, luscious texture. Soft, creamy and spreadable, it is used in many Italian desserts and as an accompaniment to a dessert of fresh fruit.
mozzarella soft, spun-curd cheese; originating in southern Italy where it was traditionally made from water-buffalo milk, now, generally, manufactured from cow milk. It is the most popular pizza cheese because of its low-melting point and elasticity when heated (used for texture rather than flavour).

parmesan also known as parmigiano; is a hard, grainy cow-milk cheese that originated in the parma region of Italy. Can be grated or flaked and used for pasta, salads and soups. Reggiano is the best parmesan, aged for a minimum 2 years and made only in the Italian region of Emilia-Romagna.
ricotta a soft, sweet, moist, white, cow-milk cheese with a low fat content (about 8.5 per cent) and a slightly grainy texture. The name roughly translates as "cooked again" and refers to ricotta's manufacture from a whey that is itself a by-product of other cheese making.

CHERVIL also known as cicily; mildly fennel-flavoured herb with curly dark-green leaves.

CHICKPEAS also called garbanzos, hummus or channa; an irregularly round, sandy-coloured legume used extensively in Mediterranean, Indian and Hispanic cooking. Has a firm texture, even after cooking, a floury mouth-feel and robust nutty flavour; available canned or dried (the latter need several hours reconstituting in cold water before being used).

CHILLIES available in many different types and sizes, both fresh and dried. Generally the smaller the chilli, the hotter it is; use rubber gloves when seeding and chopping fresh chillies as they can burn your skin.
dried flakes deep-red, dehydrated chilli slices and whole seeds; use in cooking or as a condiment for sprinkling over cooked foods.
red thai small, medium hot and bright red.

CINNAMON available both in the piece (called sticks or quills) and ground into powder; one of the world's most common spices, used universally as a sweet, fragrant flavouring for both sweet and savoury foods.

COCOA POWDER unsweetened, dried, roasted, ground, cocoa beans.

COFFEE-FLAVOURED LIQUEUR an alcoholic syrup distilled from wine or brandy and flavoured with coffee. Use Tia Maria, Kahlua or any generic brand.

CORNFLOUR also known as cornstarch. Available made from corn or wheat (wheaten cornflour, gluten-free, gives a lighter texture in cakes); used as a thickening agent in cooking.

GLOSSARY

COUSCOUS a fine, grain-like cereal product made from semolina; from the countries of North Africa. A semolina flour and water dough is sieved then dehydrated to produce minuscule even-sized pellets of couscous; it is rehydrated by steaming or with the addition of a warm liquid and swells to three or four times its original size.

CREAM (minimum fat content 18%), also known as single cream.

CUMIN also known as zeera or comino; is the dried seed of a plant related to parsley family having a spicy, nutty flavour. Available in seed form or dried and ground.

CURRANTS, DRIED dried tiny, almost black raisins so-named from the grape type native to Corinth, Greece; most often used in jams, jellies and sauces (the best-known of which is the English cumberland sauce). These are not the same as fresh currants, which are the fruit of a plant in the gooseberry family.

DATES fruit of the date palm tree, eaten fresh or dried, on their own or in prepared dishes. About 4cm to 6cm in length, oval and plump, thin-skinned, with a honey-sweet flavour and sticky texture.

EGGPLANT purple-skinned vegetable also known as aubergine. can be purchased char-grilled in jars.

FENNEL also known as finocchio or anise; a crunchy green vegetable slightly resembling celery that's eaten raw in salads, fried as an accompaniment, or used as an ingredient n pasta sauces, soups and sauce. Also the name given to the dried seeds of the plant, which have a stronger licorice flavour.

FLOUR
plain an all-purpose flour, made from wheat.
self-raising plain flour sifted with baking powder in the proportion of 1 cup flour to 2 teaspoons baking powder.

GINGER also known as green or root ginger; the thick gnarled root of a tropical plant. Can be kept, peeled, covered with dry sherry, in a jar and refrigerated, or frozen in an airtight container. *Ground ginger*, also known as powdered ginger, is used as a flavouring in cakes, pies and puddings and cannot be substituted for fresh ginger.

KALAMATA OLIVES small, sharp-tasting, brine-cured black olives.

KIPFLER POTATO small, finger-shaped, nutty flavour; great baked and in salads.

LENTILS (red, brown, yellow) dried pulses often identified by and named after their colour.

MAYONNAISE, WHOLE EGG commercial mayonnaise of high quality made with whole eggs and labelled as such; some prepared mayonnaises substitute emulsifiers such as food starch, cellulose gel or other thickeners to achieve the same thick and creamy consistency. Must be refrigerated once opened.

MUSCATEL also known as muscat grapes; used to make the sweet dessert wine having the same name. This grape variety is superb eaten fresh; when dried, its distinctively musty flavour goes well with cheese, chocolate, pork and game.

MUSTARD, AMERICAN-STYLE bright yellow in colour, a sweet mustard containing mustard seeds, sugar, salt, spices and garlic. Serve with hot dogs and hamburgers.

NUTMEG a strong and very pungent spice ground from the dried nut of an evergreen tree native to Indonesia. Usually found ground but the flavour is more intense from a whole nut, available from spice shops, so it's best to grate your own.

OIL
cooking spray we use a cholesterol-free cooking spray made from canola oil.
olive made from ripened olives. *Extra virgin* and *virgin* are the first and second press of the olives and are, therefore, considered the best; the *extra light* or *light* name on other types refers to taste not fat levels.
vegetable any of a number of oils sourced from plants rather than animal fats.

ONIONS
brown and white these can be used interchangeably. Their pungent flesh adds flavour to a vast range of dishes.
green also known as scallion or, incorrectly, shallot; an immature onion picked before the bulb has formed, having a long, bright-green edible stalk.

red also known as spanish, red spanish or bermuda onion; a sweet-flavoured, large, purple-red onion.

PANCETTA an Italian unsmoked bacon; pork belly is cured in salt and spices then rolled into a sausage shape and dried for several weeks. Used sliced or chopped, as an ingredient rather than eaten on its own; can also be used to add taste and moisture to tough or dry cuts of meat.

PAPRIKA ground dried sweet red capsicum (bell pepper); there are many grades and types available, including sweet, hot, mild and smoked.

PARSLEY, FLAT-LEAF also known as continental parsley or italian parsley.

PASTRY
fillo also known as phyllo; tissue-thin pastry sheets purchased chilled or frozen that are easy to work with and very versatile, lending themselves to both sweet and savoury dishes.
puff (ready-rolled) packaged sheets of frozen puff pastry.

PINE NUTS also known as pignoli; not really nuts, but small, cream-coloured kernels from the cones of several types of pine tree.

PISTACHIOS green, delicately flavoured nuts inside hard off-white shells. Available salted or unsalted in their shells; you can also get them shelled.

POLENTA a flour-like cereal made of ground corn (maize); similar to cornmeal but coarser and darker in colour. Also the name of the dish made from it.

PROSCIUTTO a kind of unsmoked Italian ham; salted, air-cured and aged, it is usually eaten uncooked.

QUAIL small, delicate-flavoured game birds ranging in weight from 250g to 300g; also known as partridge.

RAISINS dried sweet grapes (traditionally muscatel grapes).

ROCKET also known as arugula, rugula and rucola; peppery green leaf eaten raw in salads or used in cooking. Baby rocket leaves are smaller and less peppery.

ROSEWATER extract made from crushed rose petals; used for its aromatic quality in many sweetmeats and desserts.

SAMBAL OELEK (also spelled ulek or olek) Indonesian in origin; a salty paste made from ground chillies and vinegar.

SAUCES

fish made from pulverised salted fermented fish (most often anchovies); has a pungent smell and strong taste. Available in varying degrees of intensity; use according to taste.

soy made from fermented soy beans. Light soy sauce is light in colour but generally quite salty, while salt-reduced soy sauce contains less salt. Several variations are available in most supermarkets and Asian food stores.

Tabasco brand name of an extremely fiery sauce made from vinegar, hot red chillies and salt.

tomato also known as ketchup or catsup; a flavoured condiment made from tomatoes, vinegar and spices.

worcestershire a thin, dark-brown spicy sauce used as a seasoning and condiment.

SAVOIARDI SPONGE FINGER BISCUITS

also known as savoy biscuits, lady's fingers or sponge fingers, they are Italian-style crisp fingers made from sponge cake mixture.

SAVOY CABBAGE large, heavy head with crinkled dark-green outer leaves; a fairly mild tasting cabbage.

SEAFOOD

calamari a type of squid; substitute with baby octopus.

mussels should be bought from a fish market where there is reliably fresh fish; they must be tightly closed when bought, indicating they are alive. Before cooking, scrub the shells with a strong brush and remove the beards; discard any shells that do not open after cooking. Varieties include black and green-lip.

octopus are usually tenderised before you buy them; both octopus and squid require either long slow cooking (large molluscs) or quick cooking over high heat (small molluscs), anything in between will make the octopus tough and rubbery.

prawns also known as shrimp. Varieties include, school, king, royal red, Sydney and tiger. Can be bought uncooked (green) or cooked, with or without shells.

squid also known as calamari; a type of mollusc. Buy squid hoods to make preparation and cooking faster.

SPINACH also known as english spinach and incorrectly, silver beet. Baby spinach leaves are best eaten raw in salads; the larger leaves should be added last to soups, stews and stir-fries, and should be cooked until barely wilted.

SUGAR

brown extremely soft, fine granulated sugar retaining molasses for its characteristic colour and flavour.

caster also known as superfine or finely granulated table sugar.

icing also known as confectioners' sugar or powdered sugar; pulverised granulated sugar crushed together with a small amount (about 3 per cent) of cornflour.

white granulated table sugar; also known as crystal sugar.

SULTANAS also known as golden raisins; dried seedless white grapes.

TAHINI sesame seed paste available from Middle Eastern food stores; most often used in Lebanese recipes such as hummus.

TOMATO

canned whole peeled tomatoes in natural juices; available crushed, chopped or diced, sometimes unsalted or reduced salt. Used in recipes with the juice.

egg also called plum or roma, these are smallish, ovel-shaped tomatoes.

paste triple-concentrated tomato puree used to flavour soups, stews, sauces and casseroles.

puree canned pureed tomatoes (not tomato paste); substitute with fresh peeled and pureed tomatoes.

semi-dried partially dried tomato pieces in olive oil; softer and juicier than sun-dried, these are not a preserve thus do not keep as long as sun-dried.

sun-dried we use sun-dried tomatoes packaged in oil, unless otherwise stated.

truss small vine-ripened tomatoes with vine still attached.

TURMERIC also known as kamin. Is a rhizome related to galangal and ginger; must be grated or pounded to release its somewhat acrid aroma and pungent flavour.

VANILLA

bean dried, long, thin pod from a tropical golden orchid grown in central and South America and Tahiti; the minuscule black seeds inside the bean are used to impart a luscious vanilla flavour in baking and desserts. Place a whole bean in a jar of sugar to make the vanilla sugar often called for in recipes; a bean can be used three or four times before losing its flavour.

extract obtained from vanilla beans infused in water; a non-alcoholic version of essence.

VINEGAR

balsamic made from a regional wine of white Trebbiano grapes specially processed then aged in antique wooden casks to give the exquisite pungent flavour. Originally from Modena, Italy, there are now many balsamic vinegars on the market ranging in pungency and quality depending on how long they have been aged.

cider made from fermented apples.

red wine made from red wine.

WONTON WRAPPERS made of flour, egg and water, are found in the refrigerated or freezer section of Asian food shops and many supermarkets. These come in different thicknesses and shapes. Thin wrappers work best in soups, while the thicker ones are best for frying; and the choice of round or square, small or large is dependent on the recipe.

YOGURT we use plain full-cream yogurt in our recipes unless otherwise stated.

ZUCCHINI also known as courgette; small, pale- or dark-green, yellow or white vegetable belonging to the squash family. Harvested when young, its edible flowers can be stuffed then deep-fried or oven-baked.

MEASURES

One Australian metric measuring cup holds approximately 250ml; one Australian metric tablespoon holds 20ml; one Australian metric teaspoon holds 5ml.

The difference between one country's measuring cups and another's is within a two- or three-teaspoon variance, and will not affect your cooking results. North America, New Zealand and the United Kingdom use a 15ml tablespoon.

All cup and spoon measurements are level. The most accurate way of measuring dry ingredients is to weigh them. When measuring liquids, use a clear glass or plastic jug with the metric markings.

We use large eggs with an average weight of 60g.

DRY MEASURES

METRIC	IMPERIAL
15g	½oz
30g	1oz
60g	2oz
90g	3oz
125g	4oz (¼lb)
155g	5oz
185g	6oz
220g	7oz
250g	8oz (½lb)
280g	9oz
315g	10oz
345g	11oz
375g	12oz (¾lb)
410g	13oz
440g	14oz
470g	15oz
500g	16oz (1lb)
750g	24oz (1½lb)
1kg	32oz (2lb)

LIQUID MEASURES

METRIC	IMPERIAL
30ml	1 fluid oz
60ml	2 fluid oz
100ml	3 fluid oz
125ml	4 fluid oz
150ml	5 fluid oz (¼ pint/1 gill)
190ml	6 fluid oz
250ml	8 fluid oz
300ml	10 fluid oz (½ pint)
500ml	16 fluid oz
600ml	20 fluid oz (1 pint)
1000ml (1 litre)	1¾ pints

LENGTH MEASURES

METRIC	IMPERIAL
3mm	⅛in
6mm	¼in
1cm	½in
2cm	¾in
2.5cm	1in
5cm	2in
6cm	2½in
8cm	3in
10cm	4in
13cm	5in
15cm	6in
18cm	7in
20cm	8in
23cm	9in
25cm	10in
28cm	11in
30cm	12in (1ft)

OVEN TEMPERATURES

These oven temperatures are only a guide for conventional ovens.
For fan-forced ovens, check the manufacturer's manual.

	°C (CELSIUS)	°F (FAHRENHEIT)	GAS MARK
Very slow	120	250	½
Slow	150	275-300	1-2
Moderately slow	160	325	3
Moderate	180	350-375	4-5
Moderately hot	200	400	6
Hot	220	425-450	7-8
Very hot	240	475	9

CONVERSION CHART

ARE YOU MISSING SOME OF THE WORLD'S FAVOURITE COOKBOOKS?

The Australian Women's Weekly Cookbooks are available from bookshops, cookshops, supermarkets and other stores all over the world. You can also buy direct from the publisher, using the order form below.

TITLE	RRP	QTY	TITLE	RRP	QTY
Asian, Meals in Minutes	£6.99		Indian Cooking Class	£6.99	
Babies & Toddlers Good Food	£6.99		Japanese Cooking Class	£6.99	
Barbecue Meals In Minutes	£6.99		Just For One	£6.99	
Beginners Cooking Class	£6.99		Kids' Birthday Cakes	£6.99	
Beginners Simple Meals	£6.99		Kids Cooking	£6.99	
Beginners Thai	£6.99		Kids' Cooking Step-by-Step	£6.99	
Best Food	£6.99		Lean Food	£6.99	
Best Food Desserts	£6.99		Low-carb, Low-fat	£6.99	
Best Food Fast	£6.99		Low-fat Feasts	£6.99	
Best Food Mains	£6.99		Low-fat Food For Life	£6.99	
Cafe Classics	£6.99		Low-fat Meals in Minutes	£6.99	
Cakes, Bakes & Desserts	£6.99		Main Course Salads	£6.99	
Cakes Biscuits & Slices	£6.99		Mexican	£6.99	
Cakes Cooking Class	£6.99		Middle Eastern Cooking Class	£6.99	
Caribbean Cooking	£6.99		Midweek Meals in Minutes	£6.99	
Casseroles	£6.99		Moroccan & the Foods of North Africa	£6.99	
Casseroles & Slow-Cooked Classics	£6.99		Muffins, Scones & Breads	£6.99	
Cheap Eats	£6.99		New Casseroles	£6.99	
Cheesecakes: baked and chilled	£6.99		New Classics	£6.99	
Chicken	£6.99		New Curries	£6.99	
Chicken Meals in Minutes	£6.99		New Finger Food	£6.99	
Chinese Cooking Class	£6.99		New French Food	£6.99	
Christmas Cooking	£6.99		New Salads	£6.99	
Chocolate	£6.99		Party Food and Drink	£6.99	
Cocktails	£6.99		Pasta Meals in Minutes	£6.99	
Cooking for Friends	£6.99		Potatoes	£6.99	
Cupcakes & Fairycakes	£6.99		Salads: Simple, Fast & Fresh	£6.99	
Detox	£6.99		Saucery	£6.99	
Dinner Beef	£6.99		Sauces Salsas & Dressings	£6.99	
Dinner Lamb	£6.99		Sensational Stir-Fries	£6.99	
Dinner Seafood	£6.99		Slim	£6.99	
Easy Curry	£6.99		Soup	£6.99	
Easy Spanish-Style	£6.99		Stir-fry	£6.99	
Essential Soup	£6.99		Superfoods for Exam Success	£6.99	
Foods of the Mediterranean	£6.99		Sweet Old Fashioned Favourites	£6.99	
Foods That Fight Back	£6.99		Tapas Mezze Antipasto & other bites	£6.99	
Fresh Food Fast	£6.99		Thai Cooking Class	£6.99	
Fresh Food for Babies & Toddlers	£6.99		Traditional Italian	£6.99	
Good Food Fast	£6.99		Vegetarian Meals in Minutes	£6.99	
Great Lamb Cookbook	£6.99		Vegie Food	£6.99	
Greek Cooking Class	£6.99		Wicked Sweet Indulgences	£6.99	
Grills	£6.99		Wok, Meals in Minutes	£6.99	
Healthy Heart Cookbook	£6.99		TOTAL COST:	£	

Mr/Mrs/Ms _____

Address _____

_____ Postcode _____

Day time phone _____ Email* (optional) _____

I enclose my cheque/money order for £ _____

or please charge £ _____

to my: ☐ Access ☐ Mastercard ☐ Visa ☐ Diners Club

PLEASE NOTE: WE DO NOT ACCEPT SWITCH OR ELECTRON CARDS

Card number ☐☐☐☐ ☐☐☐☐ ☐☐☐☐ ☐☐☐☐

Expiry date _____ 3 digit security code *(found on reverse of card)* _____

Cardholder's name_____ Signature _____

To order: Mail or fax – photocopy or complete the order form above, and send your credit card details or cheque payable to: Australian Consolidated Press (UK), 10 Scirocco Close, Moulton Park Office Village, Northampton NN3 6AP, phone (+44) (0) 1604 642 200 fax (+44) (0) 1604 642 300, e-mail books@acpuk. com or order online at www.acpuk.com
Non-UK residents: We accept the credit cards listed on the coupon, or cheques, drafts or International Money Orders payable in sterling and drawn on a UK bank. Credit card charges are at the exchange rate current at the time of payment.
Postage and packing UK: Add £1.00 per order plus 50p per book.
Postage and packing overseas: Add £2.00 per order plus £1.00 per book.
All pricing current at time of going to press and subject to change/availability.
Offer ends 31.12.2007

* By including your email address, you consent to receipt of any email regarding this magazine, and other emails which inform you of ACP's other publications, products, services and events, and to promote third party goods and services you may be interested in.